How to Make a Good Marriage Great

How to Make a Good Marriage Great

Victor B. Cline, Ph.D.

Bookcraft
Salt Lake City, Utah

Library of Congress Catalog Card Number: 96-85097
ISBN 1-57008-255-3

Revised edition
First Printing, 1996

Printed in the United States of America

Contents

3 *When Divorce Is the Only Way*

4 *Summing Up*

Acknowledgments

Grateful acknowledgment is made to Patty Cannon and Dr. D. Corydon Hammond for reviewing portions of the manuscript and making insightful and helpful comments.

A special debt is particularly due to Lee and Lorna Franke, Dean and Joan Connolly, Jim and Terrie Telford, Lynn and Barbra Brasher, and Cordell and Liz Smith, whose lives and personal sacrifice in connection with the Marriage Enrichment seminars led by my wife, Lois, and me served as an inspiration for this book. I would also like to acknowledge the remarkable vision and contributions of John and Diane Hart, who helped bring the Marriage Enrichment program to the Seattle area.

Lois and I are forever in debt to all the gracious and loving people who gave us Marriage Encounter, a remarkable and joyous experience, along with David and Vera Mace, who influenced our lives and served as role models for us all in making contributions whose value can never be fully appreciated and whose ideas and theories permeate this book.

Dr. Carlfred Broderick has proved a great treasure of ideas and techniques, from which I have borrowed shamelessly and liberally in my counseling practice as well as in this book. Acknowledgment is also due to Sharon Arnold and Marvin Gardner for their most helpful editorial contributions.

Cory H. Maxwell, as editorial manager for the publisher, is also to be thanked for his kind and wise support, especially in bringing into print this second edition through Bookcraft. I am also very appreciative of the highly competent and sensitive job of editing by the Bookcraft staff.

And finally, I express love and affection to my wife, Lois, who has been with me on a great journey of discovery and joy. She and our children—Russell, Janice, Robyn, Christopher, Richard, Connie, Paul, Julie, and Rebecca—are the treasures of my life.

PART 1

The Grand Plan:
A Journey into Joy

CHAPTER 1

The Impossible Dream: Beginning the Journey

Frank looked half disgusted and half sad. He was telling me about his marriage. "Everybody—I mean everybody—likes me. That is, everybody but my wife! She treats even stray dogs and strangers better than me. I provide a good income. I don't cheat. I've never hit her. I rarely put her down. I'm a good father to the kids. And I still love her. But somehow I can't seem to please her. She's always mad at me. I can't handle the constant rejection.

"I used to be a happy guy. I'm losing my confidence. Why do I stay in there and like a fool keep trying? Maybe it's the kids. I really love them. I guess the problem is I hate to admit defeat. But how much longer can I hang on? Or do I even want to?" He shook his head in confusion and despair.

The Workaholic Husband

When I first met Jerry he was extremely depressed. His wife had kicked him out of the house he had built with his own hands. He had not seen his two preschool sons for more than ten days—

and they were the light of his life. Because he was still in love with his wife, Linda's rejection of him cut very deeply. He knew that he was partially responsible. His workaholic tendencies—especially weekends—had gradually created a deep gulf in their relationship. Linda felt very ignored and abandoned at times—left, so it seemed, to raise these two high-energy boys by herself. He was never there. No movies together. Never dinner out. Just an exhausted, short-tempered husband who complained of an awful work load that never seemed to let up.

She saw him only at his worst. Her tears and pleas were ignored. Finally, in desperation she insisted he leave. It was then that he somehow found time for counseling. As he explored all his options he decided to rearrange his priorities. He chose to place his family first. He saw that no success in his work could ever compensate for the loss of those he loved most and on whom his happiness was most dependent. As he began rearranging his schedule to be home more, he found, surprisingly, that his job efficiency increased—even as he spent less time at it. He found that with clear intention and focused energy he was able to "have it all"—something he had not believed possible before.

Kathy bit her lip. Tears suddenly came to her eyes. She couldn't hold them back. She struggled to find words to express her pain.

"He left! He just walked out! He never said anything! And the baby's due in five weeks. I didn't even know there was anything that wrong. I thought we had a good marriage. Ten pretty decent years. We never really fought or quarreled much. I don't know what happened. He wouldn't discuss it. What went wrong? I just don't know. What do I do now?"

Making It or Not Making It

Close to half of the couples marrying today will experience divorce in their lifetime. The other half who do keep their marriages together will do so not because of an absence of problems or stress in their relationship, but because they have developed the ability to resolve problems and move through them successfully.

Good marriages are not problem free. In fact, I suspect that there are really no great differences in the number and severity of problems in the marriages of those who divorce and those who do not. The difference is in the individuals' commitment, energy, and skill in creating joy and continuing love in their relationship—despite whatever disasters booby-trap them along the way.

I have seen many once-excellent marriages fail because the couples lacked the necessary problem-solving skills. And I've seen other marriages where two quite mismatched people *did* make it work and work gloriously.

The Therapist as Sherlock Holmes

I have been a psychotherapist and family and marriage counselor for several decades. Each problem that comes through my door is in many ways unique and creates its own sort of pain for the owner. I see myself as a kind of Sherlock Holmes whose task is to find and illuminate the core problem and then discover the strategies and solutions that are most likely to help. Each problem has a dynamic core that is somewhat different from any other. An accurate diagnosis and understanding is absolutely crucial if I am to be of help and if creative solutions are to be found.

For example, with one couple I saw, the husband complained bitterly about his wife's abusive temper, assaultiveness, and total unreasonableness. At times he felt she hated him for no apparent reason. If it weren't for the children, he confided to me, he would have left her long ago. It turned out that her problem was primarily biological. She had a particularly nasty case of premenstrual syndrome which rendered her vulnerable to any kind of stress during the two weeks before menstruation. She knew she was difficult at those times and felt guilty about it but was unable to control the awful feelings that surged through her. Ordinary marriage counseling would not have touched this problem. Progesterone and a special diet and exercise program made a dramatic difference in Linda as well as in her marital relationship.

There are many reasons for divorce. Sometimes it is simply immaturity and selfishness on the part of one or both partners.

Each knows how to take but is not willing or able to give much. When this occurs, somebody's emotional well eventually runs dry, and no couple can survive this loss very long. Something has to eventually come in to replenish the supply in order to feed and nurture the relationship.

Sometimes one of the partners is acutely neurotic or paranoid. They perceive not only the world but also their partner through a grossly distorted lens. This greatly complicates the communication between the pair. They grope with words to negotiate through the problems but too often end up in confusion and frustration.

Shadows from the Past

Sometimes shadows from a malignant past haunt the present relationship. The wife brings her fears and hatred of a difficult father to her marriage. She unconsciously punishes her husband for her father's tyranny, infidelity, alcoholism, oppression, or inability to love her. Or the husband had a domineering, angry, or rejecting mother. It is a miracle he ever married at all. But one thing is for sure, he'll let no woman ever do to him what his mother did to him and poor old Dad. In such cases there is usually a deep residual anger toward all women buried in the unconscious. And the wife pays and pays for her husband's mother's mistakes. But then his mother was herself a victim of an abused, tortured childhood. She is illustrating the fact that emotional illnesses are highly contagious and pass down through the generations.

Of course, it works the other way, too. If one has had the advantage of a good relationship with a parent of the opposite gender, it can strengthen a person to tolerate a difficult spouse through harried and stressful times. Supported by such happy childhood experiences, a husband or wife is prepared to expect good things. Their unconscious tells them, "Better days are ahead." And amazingly they continue to excuse their spouse's bad behavior, saying, "This is just temporary. She doesn't really mean it. When she's mean it's not really her." Their psyche has been programmed to have positive expectations about females (or males). It takes quite awhile to scramble these expectations.

Thus one partner can tolerate quite a bit of obnoxiousness in the other before finally getting the message, "My spouse *really* is messed up—and is not going to change easily." But the miracle that I witness daily is seeing people change. They can heal. They can be transformed. I believe that within most of us is a natural tendency to "get better," analogous to our body's remarkable, automatic self-healing system. This doesn't happen instantly or without effort. But it still can happen. I find that most people prefer happiness and good relationships and will move in that direction given half a chance.

Why So Much Pain?

I looked at my wife, Lois, crumpled asleep on our queen-sized bed. It was 3:00 A.M. I had just returned by a late-night flight from a business trip to Panama City, Florida. She had given her all, day after day, year after year, in raising our nine kids and being my wife. The lines of fatigue were gently etched across her face. I thought of the thousand nights she instantly awoke when one of the children suddenly choked, gasped, or cried out in their sleep. I thought of our joys and triumphs, but also of the struggle, losses, and, sometimes, pain. Why did that have to be? Why couldn't we just find and marry the right person and live forever in peace without struggle? Wasn't God pro-marriage? Didn't He create the family? Why did He permit us to suffer so much at times in our relationships?

I slipped into my pajamas, then slid into bed, cuddling my arms around her. She reflexively moved into my embrace as she always did, even in a deep sleep. Before my tired mind slipped into oblivion I vaguely thought about the number 127. One hundred and twenty-seven. It had a special meaning for me. This was the number of key traits that I had discovered were related to success in marriage. I had come across this in doing the early literature review on my marriage research project for the National Institutes of Mental Health. I would frequently tell couples in counseling about this. I would explain to them that no matter how carefully they chose their partner, there would always be some areas out of those 127 where there would be mismatch or incompatibility. No exceptions.

Even in the best marriages I have invariably found that there are always areas of conflict. In many years of counseling and living, I have learned that every husband has grounds for divorce! But so does every wife—in all marriages, even the very best. Every spouse has a list of marital grievances. And this should be expected. See it as an exciting challenge or great opportunity for growth, not as an excuse to run away. I see too many couples getting divorced for trivial reasons. These are divorces that need never happen. Despite the pain, most of their problems are solvable. Little do they realize that the odds of making it in their next relationship are no better and possibly even worse.

The Seventh Wife

I then remembered clearly that warm August afternoon when a wealthy businessman came to see me. He was greatly upset because his seventh marriage was breaking up after only one month.

"Doctor, this last one, she is worse than all that went before. How could this have happened to me? I dated her a full year. I thought she was finally the one!" Then he said something that burned into my memory, something I'll never forget. "You know," he reflected ruefully, "I should have stayed with my first wife. Yes, we had a few problems and differences. But they really weren't that great. I know we could have worked them out. I mistakenly thought that I could do better. I let her go."

This gentleman is now paying huge sums in alimony and child support all over the country because of his indulgence.

I knew the basic truth of his cry of anguish. Every time a person marries or remarries, he or she faces a whole new set of adjustments and challenges. So what else is new? And who said that life was easy or that anything really great in our lives could come without a price or many sacrifices? The alternative to marriage, with its accompanying challenges and struggle, is loneliness. Ask anybody in the singles' world about that. One-third of adults in our country are single now. I see many singles in my practice. It is not an easy world to live in.

Hazards of Men Being Alone

Researcher-writer George Gilder, in his book *Naked Nomads: Unmarried Men in America*, has reviewed data from many studies and sources which suggest that being alone, especially for men, is associated with much higher rates of physical illness, depression, accidents, suicide, mental illness, and lower income. To be male and alone is risky. And if one thinks this merely proves that the accident-prone and mentally ill tend not to marry as frequently, the statistics suggest that when married men divorce or become widowers they also quickly become vulnerable to all of these problems.

There is an elemental truth expressed in the book of Genesis where it suggests that it is not good for man (or woman) to be alone. As a psychologist and couple counselor, I concur with this. Without a partner our lives are less complete emotionally, psychologically, and spiritually. Sure, we can survive, but we still aren't complete. While this may offend some singles, it is still true. However, even in mentioning this, I think it is important to realize that it is better to be alone than to be emotionally or physically abused in a destructive, degrading marriage, especially where there are major values differences.

Again I looked at my sleeping wife, and I knew that she was good for me. She kept me honest. There was a continuing kind of feedback and honesty in our relationship that kept me humble and responsible whether I liked it or not. I needed her, and I knew she needed me. We gave each other balance and strength.

She could cry. She could pout, become angry, lose control. I knew her moods and cycles. She knew I loved her despite and maybe partly because of her humanness. But with a certain kind of existential equity or justice, she knew most of my failures, limitations, pettiness, and inadequacies and still loved me despite them. We were good for each other. But it took a lot of years to forge this kind of relationship. There were repeated struggles, disappointments, doubts, and pain, as well as joy and periods of peace and delight. But underlying all of this was a core commitment to the relationship.

Any Couple Can Make It?

A local marriage counselor once said in a lecture I attended, "In any marriage, any couple can make it—if they want to." I had initially been a little irritated, maybe angered, by such a bold statement. It seemed rather ridiculous! But over the years I have reluctantly come nearer and nearer to agreeing with him. Again and again I see mismatched couples making it and others who have nearly everything in their favor, but lacking commitment (or maybe because of immaturity and selfishness), breaking up and not making it.

Miracles can happen. But the miracle has to be found partly in the energy, will, and choice of the two partners.

I have seen cold, nagging wives turn into sensuous, noncritical lovers after many years of struggle and disappointment. The change was usually occasioned by a crisis in their relationship. Old habits were broken. They made a decision to love. To change. To be something greater than they were before. I have also seen abusive men become tender and considerate. It was not easy. But it happened. They made a decision to love, to change, to do whatever was necessary to preserve the relationship that they now valued and saw a potential for growth in. They believed it could happen. They made it happen.

Couple counseling is the toughest kind of work I know. It is also the most exciting, rewarding, exasperating, and challenging adventure that a therapist can ever engage in. I do it because I know that I can affect far more lives this way. Hour for hour I can be more helpful doing this than I could doing anything else I know. Some of these battles we win. And some we lose.

I am not always sure why.

I Have Never Seen a Pretty Divorce

Approximately a hundred years ago the divorce rate in the United States was about 0.3 couples per year per population of one hundred thousand. In the 1980s it was 5.3, an almost twentyfold or 2,000 percent increase.

In actual numbers the increase is much greater. In just two decades we went from around three hundred thousand divorces per year to 1.2 million. Here we are talking about 2.4 million adults calling it quits each year. If you include the kids, this figure may reach over 4 million people who are yearly going through the misery of a broken home and family. In one decade, that would be nearly 40 million people.

I have never seen a pretty divorce. They all hurt. And with some the hurt and conflict continue for many years undiminished, especially where children and custody are involved.

Currently our national divorce rate is the highest of all of the major nations of the world. We lead the pack. One-half of the children born this year will spend a good part of their growing years in a one-parent family.

The purpose of this book is to present what I know about how to maintain your marriage relationship, how to increase affection and improve communication skills, and how to heal old wounds and dissolve emotional scar tissue. If you are not yet married or are divorced, I have some highly practical suggestions for picking a loving spouse who may be right for you (see chapter 22).

The Role of Ecclesiastical Leaders

Being a member of The Church of Jesus Christ of Latter-day Saints, I see and work with a number of Latter-day Saint couples in my clinical practice. I find that most of these have previously consulted together with their ecclesiastical leaders—bishops, stake presidents—about their marital problems (and those I see who are of other faiths have sometimes talked with their respective clergymen). Some of these Latter-day Saint couples have been given the recommendation to seek out some focused marriage counseling from a counselor who shares their spiritual and religious values.

Thus in the ideal case, the healing of the couple's wounds becomes a team effort: the couple, the therapist, and the priesthood leader. As the couple's spiritual leader and steward, a bishop or a stake president may do certain kinds of things that only such a priesthood leader can do—such as call the couple to repentance or, if necessary, temporarily suspend their temple recommends. This is beyond the professional counselor's scope or prerogative. And this I always support and endorse. There are certain things a bishop can uniquely do to contribute to a couple's well-being; and there are other things that a professional counselor can do to help them work through their differences. Each has a place in the scheme of things leading to eventual healing. But above all the couple have their free agency, and they alone must assume responsibility for seeking out healing solutions to their problems.

No Training for Marriage

Marriage is one thing that we have never been given any real training for. To drive a car most of us have to test for skill and knowledge. In many states driver education is mandatory. But to get married all one needs in most states is a few dollars. And it is doubtful that this situation will change much in the future, for we cherish individual choice and freedom above nearly all other values. This even includes the freedom to live in misery and make colossal errors in choosing whom we marry.

Jonathon Freedman, author of *Happy People,* studied a sample of one hundred thousand Americans and found that the most important factor in human happiness was "loving" and "being loved." He concluded, "A vast majority of our population seemed to find happiness in marriage and to be unhappy if they remain single."

Two other researchers, Norman Glenn and Charles Weaver, reviewed data from six U.S. national surveys on what factors most contributed to one's overall happiness. In their sophisticated and lengthy analysis of these various studies, they found that "for all race/sex subpopulations, a happy marriage seems virtually necessary for a high level of happiness." Or to put it another way, for most adults, happiness depends more upon having a good marriage than upon anything else (including work satisfaction, financial success, health, friendships, housing, etc.). So, if happiness is important to you, you have to put together a good marriage, or better yet, make the good marriage you now have great! Let us explore how. Let us share all we know. Couples are doing it every day. Why not you?

CHAPTER 2

What Every Wife Wants
from Her Husband

Every once in a while when I am at a movie, concert, or lecture, I will see a couple in front of me or to the side somewhere who generate a certain electricity in their presence together. You can see it in the sparkle in the wife's eyes, the slight trace of smile on her lips, and sense of deep satisfaction and vitality in her face. As she ever so slightly brushes her arm against her husband's body or touches his neck or shoulder with the tips of her fingers, he draws toward her like steel filings to a magnet. He has a look of contentment and peace on his face. The wife is clearly someone who is being loved and experiencing deep fulfillment.

What is it that most women want from their mates? What is it that really sustains them? I have asked that question many thousands of times and have witnessed many tears shed by emotionally starved wives living in unfulfilling relationships. I would like to share with you the best of what I have seen and heard.

1. Every wife that I have ever interviewed has expressed a major desire for her man to *cherish, want, and need* her. She has to feel that she is extremely important in his life. She

needs to know that whether she lives or dies *does* make all the difference in the world to him. She needs to somehow get that from him. Her man can be flawed in a lot of ways—but not here.

2. *Be a good communicator.* Women are very verbal. They like to talk. This is their world. This is the indoor sport that most are incredibly good at. They thrive on social intercourse. Most men are alien to the art of conversation as women know it. But effective communication between husband and wife is the key to a healthy marriage. It means they can negotiate and resolve differences. But, best of all, they can share their deepest feelings—be great friends. When women strike up relationships outside of their marriage commitment it is almost always with the kind of male who can talk, whose words bolster their flagging egos and make them feel like the center of the universe. Wives want partners who can communicate!

3. *Be a responsible, stable provider.* Whether the wife works or not is irrelevant. She still wants a husband who can make it out in the world and who has the smarts and willingness to earn sufficient income to pay most of the bills. He needs to have his act together, to be able to make things happen, to be dependable in following through on commitments. Part of her sense of security in the marriage stems from his strength, integrity, solidness, good judgment, and ability to handle stress and to be a good provider.

4. *Be a good lover*—in the broadest sense of the word. This means being affectionate, romantic, exciting. While positive sex may be included here, it is not a necessary requirement of a loving encounter.

5. *Be trustworthy.* He is loyal—not open to emotional involvement with other women. He has personal integrity.

6. *Build her self-esteem.* He has the talent and chooses to make her feel like a worthwhile individual. He lifts her up when she is down. This also means that he is *positive* in his interaction and communication with her at least 90 percent of the time. If he has a concern or constructive criticism, of course it is important that he bring it up—but *always* in a tender and responsible way, as he would expect from her. Being a chronic criticizing grump is like pouring vinegar into a fresh quart of milk. It spoils the whole thing. A husband needs to promote his wife's best qualities, and every wife needs to sense lots of positive emotional support from that one person who means the most to her.

7. *Share the work load at home.* The husband must not be afraid to change a messy diaper, wash a few dishes, vacuum some bedrooms as the occasion demands, and either do or delegate outside work, cleanup, or other tasks that need to be done. He will be more involved in these activities, of course, if his wife works full-time outside the home.

8. *Be a good parent, a true father* to the kids. The husband needs to fill his role in this important area in a way that the kids prosper and sense his solid emotional support. Every mother has a special attachment to her children—she nurtured each of them for nine months in her womb. When she sees her husband treat them with consideration, this bonds her feelings of affection to him even more.

CHAPTER 3

What Every Husband
Wants from His Wife

I am convinced that there is a difference sometimes between what a man says he wants and what he *really* wants from his wife. This chapter deals with what, in my judgment, most husbands really want. Then for each particular man there will be some unique needs that you, his partner, will discover as you love and live with him. If you pay attention and listen to him, you will discover these special needs. Fill his cup, and he will be yours forever.

1. *Accept and approve the husband.* I cannot overemphasize the importance of this. Most husbands are out there every day fighting the dragons, and when they come home at night they want their wives to be proud of them, appreciate their contributions and sacrifices, believe in them—be on their side. The loving, understanding wife is the husband's shelter in the storm. She should be the one who patches up bruises, nurtures him, and heals and builds his battered ego, and sees and treats him as a prince in their kingdom. He needs to understand that he is number one in her life above all other people.

I interview a lot of "other women" who are involved with husbands in failing marriages. These are the women whom the husband gets tangled up with when his marriage isn't working. And surprisingly few of them are the slender, good-looking sex kittens common to the television stereotype. Yet they do have one quality that makes them very attractive to a disenchanted husband. These women genuinely accept and appreciate him. They are not critical. They approve of him. They validate him as a man, a person, a human being. It is easy to understand this attraction in a man carrying a lot of stress in his life, especially where he and his wife are experiencing long-term coldness or constant bickering in their marriage. Or where the wife is chronically angry with him, criticizing him, and repeatedly rejecting him, for whatever reasons. Such a wife risks destroying any hope of reestablishing a warm, intimate marital relationship.

I see some marriages where the husband does 95 percent of the things a husband should do. But when he fails in the other 5 percent of what his wife expects of him, she may, as punishment, reject him in major ways. Or she may be abusive (like her mother was to her father) in order to shape him up. So she gets caught up in a cycle of constant criticism.

I remember one husband whose stomach would begin to knot up every time he came up the walk to his front door. He knew he would catch all sorts of grief for something—anything—when he got inside. And, sure enough, he always did. Eventually he left the marriage. Many husbands feel unloved and unappreciated in their own homes by the very person whose love they need the most. It becomes a negative cycle. Soon the husband withdraws, becomes cool (or angry), stops nurturing his wife, and everyone loses. But, of course, it does not have to stay this way. Usually all it takes is for just one partner to turn it around, to break the self-destructive pattern. But at least one partner has to make a decision to love, then change some behavior to break the pattern.

2. *Have a good-quality, positive sexual relationship.* This does not require a perfect match up or simultaneous orgasms or identical levels of desire. But it does require the wife being affectionate, showing up for the event, and participating in

a fun, romantic, adventuresome way. And this must happen often enough that he is not in pain and anger all week from constant deprivation. Three or four times a week is the *average* for most couples in the first few years of marriage. And for individual couples it will vary considerably around this mean. If either partner has a physical or psychological problem that interferes with having a positive, joyous experience here, he or she should get it taken care of immediately.

A wife also should never use sexual deprivation as a punishment. For when that happens she might well win the battle but lose the war. She also must be aware that her husband's skill as a lover will depend in part on what she teaches him about what pleases her.

While some authors and authorities may have overplayed the importance of sex, it still must be considered a vital part of the love every husband has for his wife. To engage in this most intimate and sacred embrace is a profound interpersonal experience. It is a natural way to get a high.

3. *Have personal integrity and responsibility.* To a husband, this quality in a wife means that she'll be there. She will not leave me. I can trust her. She is solid. She does not reveal family secrets. She has good morals and character. I can feel her commitment. She takes this relationship seriously. I am her one and only. And I have a deep assurance about all of this.

4. *Be a competent and effective wife and mother.* While many couples have redefined these roles somewhat since thirty or fifty years ago, the rule still applies. If one is in a more traditional marriage, it means that the wife manages the home and children (with her husband's support) competently. She gets the job done one way or another. Meals are nutritious and appetizing and on time. Clothes get cleaned, the home looks attractive, Christmas cards get mailed, and the children are loved and experience a nurturing environment.

If the wife works, or in some way marital roles are defined differently, she still carries her fair share of the load or in some way delegates it successfully.

5. *Be a friend, a good companion.* It is really great to have a wife who is fun to be around, talk to, play with, and work with—somebody who can truly be a friend. Some men are not as skilled in interpersonal relationships as are their wives; they appreciate someone who can make them feel comfortable and secure in a one-to-one relationship.

Sometimes the extreme stresses of everyday living give very little time for the husband and wife to spend much friendship time together. But if they do not take some time for themselves they can grow old together and hardly know each other. I find some couples have to go out of town to have any really good time together. The bottom line is, What are your priorities?

6. *Have open and positive communications.* Positive communications means that differences can be negotiated peacefully. It means that a thousand decisions can be made so that things can get done. It means peaceful times together.

7. Every super wife knows that there are times when she needs to *give her husband space.* He needs to be let out of the corral. He needs to have time to himself for whatever reason. She does not crowd or smother him. She lets him have some freedom, secure in the knowledge that he loves her and that this is just temporary. It may be time needed for a special project at work; a need to spend time golfing, hunting, fishing, or reading a book; or it may be taking a trip or even having some quiet time just after work as a way of unwinding. In mentioning this I am not excusing the workaholic husband who never comes home because his work never ends. That is not healthy for anyone. But a wise wife allows her husband (just as he allows her) personal space without comment or criticism.

CHAPTER 4

Communication Skills
and Beyond

Almost any survey of why marriages fail or succeed will list communication skills at the top of the list of important determinants. While innumerable books have been written on the topic and a large number of communication techniques are taught in endless seminars available to the public, I have not found most of these to be especially helpful—in real life. In this chapter I would like to share with you ideas and techniques that have worked best for me in my own life as well as with couples whom I counsel. (Also see chapter 11 on negotiating through anger and conflicts for further ideas.)

However, the problem of effective communication in marriage is a complex one. A nonverbal partner, for example, may have learned to be quiet in self-defense. As one husband told me, "My wife can out-talk me in any argument. So I just don't say much. That's how I protect myself. I may not win, but at least I don't lose." Or as one wife put it, "Yes, we talk a lot, but it's all negative. Nothing gets solved. It always winds up in a big fight and bad feelings." Thus one can "maim or kill" with a verbal exchange. Words can destroy. They can be remembered forever.

Effective communication is more than just talking: it is the type of interaction that gets a job done—solves problems, builds self-esteem, enhances the relationship, relays important messages, reinforces mutual respect, and helps bond the couple together as an effective unit.

Once my wife, Lois, and I retreated to our mountain cabin to catch up on a lengthy agenda of concerns, problems, and decisions that needed to be made. Somehow when it came time to leave we were locked into a negative cycle. Time pressure had made it difficult to deal with some of the issues between us. In addition we found that our defenses were up, which effectively blocked all progress no matter what we said or did.

Our dialogue was rational (though occasionally heated). But all we did was restate our separate opinions. Both of us felt frustrated. No progress was being made. It was ironic—we both had been trained in problem solving and successful negotiation. But somehow on this day nothing was working. The air was filled with a sense of futility and rejection, both of us adrift in the isolation of not being understood. We were discouragingly stalemated. To continue talking about some of the issues seemed only to set us back further. We drove home with bad feelings. Disappointed. We were ending our special retreat separated by an emotional chasm.

I believe that love is as much a decision as a feeling. The next morning I decided to love—no matter what our differences, frustrations, and hurts were. After the kids left for work and school, I invited Lois to spend a special hour with me. I first gave her a heartfelt letter spelling out my position in a sincere and nonblaming way. She needed to know in detail where I was, how I really felt. She read it in silence. I could tell it helped a little, even though she said, "You'll never change. That's what you said yesterday."

Then I began to talk to her spontaneously, from my heart. I let her know how much our relationship meant to me, how much I loved her, how I felt that any differences we had could always be worked out. Within a half hour the whole climate changed.

We were lovers and friends again. I had told her that I wasn't going to leave for work until our differences were resolved, our blocks worked through and removed. We went from an adversary relationship back into a loving one.

What made it happen? It was the spirit of our communication. This is sometimes called metacommunication or even nonverbal communication. It was what was in my heart and eyes. It was a deeply and genuinely felt concern and caring for my wife. This was not just for three minutes. This went for half of the morning. She *knew* I cared. She knew that I loved her—good times or bad. No matter what. She could strongly feel the change in my attitude. I was not complaining or demanding. I just cared about her and us.

I had made a decision to love *no matter what*. As I talked to my wife I didn't attack. I didn't criticize. I didn't point out her faults. I didn't defend myself. I just gave her a vision of what was possible in our future together. It was possible then for a healing to occur. A renewing of our marital bond occurred because I think we were two fairly decent people with shared values who refused to give up on each other.

Yet I know of other marital situations where this could not happen because one partner had some serious mental-health problem, was chronically drunk, or had deliberately chosen to destroy the relationship.

As Lois and I talked about why earlier we had been so blocked in our negotiations and now were free, it seemed to us that it was because of a subtle but still powerful change in attitude which now smoothed our discussions. It brought us into a unity. It changed our chemistry. We were now communicating in a climate of goodwill, trust, and caring. Another thing that I did was focus on the positive and avoid the negative. I absolutely refused to criticize, condemn, put down, or make "you are" statements.

So what I am suggesting is that just talking together may resolve nothing. What is critical, even more than the specific content, is the sense of caring for one's partner that pervades the negotiations. This is what counts most in effective communication.

While there are many programs and approaches to improving communication in marriage, I would like to summarize ten specific suggestions which I have found most beneficial:

1. Have your discussion together where kids, phone, and visitors can't disturb your train of thought. If necessary get

in the car and go behind the school, to a local park, or to an empty parking lot.

2. Allow enough time to work through important problems. Negotiating under a deadline is stressful, destructive, and often counterproductive; it diminishes the chances for a good outcome. If necessary take an "overnight" together at a local hotel.

3. Never discuss serious issues when either one of you is hungry (low blood-sugar level), way out of balance, or acutely depressed, or when the wife is in the worst part of her premenstrual cycle. In other words, communicate in prime time: when you are both rested, not hassled, and are emotionally and physically in balance.

4. Be a good listener. Hear your partner out. Don't interrupt. Let your partner have a full say. Agree on this ahead of time, so it goes both ways. After your partner has finished a thought, *paraphrase back what you have just heard.* This is called reflective listening. It is a way of verifying that you heard accurately. And also that what your partner had to say was important enough for you to pay close attention. The key thing here is *not to interrupt even if you don't agree with what you are being told or know it to be inaccurate.* Listen! Then paraphrase back. Misperceptions and inaccuracies can be corrected later. So be a good listener and don't interrupt!

5. Don't run away if things get tense or tears appear or anger emerges. Stick it out. Hold your temper. No negatives. Work through the feelings. Talk it out—peacefully. But stay there, don't leave!

6. Be honest, but do it kindly and tactfully. Be responsible and loving, *but still be honest.* If you are hurting, don't pretend differently. But you still don't have to accuse. This is

not a license to dump old garbage or bring up mistakes from the past. That's over with. We are concerned mainly about the here-and-now and the future.

7. Avoid "you" statements. Examples: "This is all *your* fault." "*You* goofed." "*You* did it." "*You* are a hateful person." "Why can't *you* ever learn?" "If *you* had just used better judgment . . ." In place of "you," use "I" statements. "I feel this way . . ." "I fear what may happen . . ." "I'm upset . . ."

8. Share *feelings*. Example: "I feel this way about our problem." Or, "I feel better about how Jenny is doing in school." Or, "I feel blue for just no reason at all."

9. Be *positive* with your partner. Give constructive, positive feedback whenever he or she pleases you (e.g., dresses nicely, handles the kids well, prepares something special to eat, or takes you to a fine dinner). Notice what your partner does that pleases you—express this! There is a law in heaven and on earth that has never been broken, the Law of Positive Reinforcement: Any behavior by your spouse that you positively reinforce will tend to be repeated! It's okay to deal with problems, just be extremely cautious about dumping criticism. Criticism can become a habit that will drive everybody away from you. Praise your spouse and children. Search out the good and keep re-minding them of it (and they will repeat it).

10. If your "discussion topic" is too hot to deal with orally—*then write about it (lovingly) in letter form.* Let your spouse read it. Then, afterward, discuss it. Or, alterna-tively, you might both write about the issue (apart, not to-gether), then at a meeting together read each other's let-ters and discuss them. This is an extremely effective way to get through your matrimonial mine field intact and un-scathed. This technique will save a great deal of grief and help you move through tough issues that are difficult to discuss.

Once when I was commiserating with a social-worker friend about eight "hard-core" couples whom we were counseling with, it just seemed to both of us as if there were no kind of therapy or technique that was capable of healing their profound differences. These marriages all appeared to be lost causes with little hope of being salvaged. After much discussion we finally decided to try an unorthodox last-ditch technique, now rarely used, called the twenty-four hour marathon. This was a long shot, to try in some way to save these marriages, for it was clear that everything else we tried was not working.

We first explained to the couples exactly what was involved. We would go to a downtown hotel, secure a comfortable suite, and engage in group therapy for twenty-four hours using some of the techniques associated with Alcoholics Anonymous. There was to be anonymity and confidentiality. First names only. We were all there to help each other. No criticism or cross talk.

It was quickly apparent that everyone there was a seasoned, battle-scarred expert in marital warfare. At this point most felt they had little to lose by trying this different approach in resolving their conflicts.

We started at seven Friday evening and went nonstop until the following Saturday evening. Delicious deli food and juices were placed on a table to one side and anyone could help themselves any time they felt hungry, but they didn't leave the room (other than bathroom breaks) or leave the group. Each couple, going in any order they chose, presented the core problems or issues that were dividing them and causing so many problems. In a gentle way they were given the space and time to work through solutions. This turned out to be a very therapeutic experience for every couple. No one was able to play dirty tricks or pull any fast ones. Though occasionally tears were shed, nobody became abusive or overly emotional or ran away as they so often did at home. Here, there was no place to go; they had to continue working on the problem. And they were fully aware that every one of the other couples were really pulling and praying for them. We noticed, after a while, a very interesting phenomenon occurring with almost every couple. When they first started talking, it appeared that it was necessary for them to vent their distress, anger, and upset for the many irritating or "wrong" things the partner had done in the past. And it wasn't until each partner had discharged this "emotional load" that they were really able then to get down to business and solve their problems. It became quickly apparent that at home the couple would get in a turmoil about almost any issue—frequently very petty—but they never stayed with it long enough to get past the "emotionally upset" phase. So nothing got resolved. And this cycle kept reoccurring year after year, with nothing ever getting worked through.

In any event, the presence of the group kept everyone responsible. And this allowed for some very powerful problem-solving experiences to occur with each couple. We found that if a couple negotiated long enough, it was possible to nearly always come up with win-win solutions to all kinds of marital differences. At home this was not usually possible because either one or both of the partners had become so gun-shy they would walk out, get mad, or cry, which only produced frustration and no solutions to anything. From this experience and several follow-ups, we saved six of the eight marriages.

Several months later I took my own wife on a private marathon—it was just she and I. A day and a half in a nearby hotel. Nice food, no interruptions. Alone together. And guess what? Exactly the same thing happened. There were some tears, strong feelings, a recital of grievances, and so on. But rather than walk out I stayed with it, knowing there would eventually be a healing resolution. And that is exactly what happened with us. It was wonderful.

You can do the same. With patience and a noncontentious spirit your marriage can be greatly blessed. Try a private "marathon."

CHAPTER 5

Sexual Love That Lasts:
What It Takes

M arital love consists of four keystone elements: friendship, romance, sex, and sacrifice. Like legs on a stool, each in its own way supports the total relationship—but one by itself can never balance the whole marriage.

Sex Is Not Enough

Gus, a twenty-eight-year-old race car driver and his wife, Sandy, had an incredible sexual chemistry. When they coupled it was like the San Francisco earthquake, the Creation, and the Fourth of July all rolled into one. But that was all. There was no romance, just self-indulgence. No friendship, no sacrifice. They used each other. They were extremely selfish, immature, narcissistic people.

Their marriage lasted barely a year; their sexual explosion burned out because of their increasing anger, irritation, and frustration with each other. They did not know how to communicate, negotiate, solve problems, support, share, or love. It ended in exhaustion, coldness, separation, and finally divorce with much mutual recrimination.

Just as one's body cannot survive on sugar, a marriage needs more than good sex. Your physical body needs full nutrition, and so does a marriage. Sex by itself can never fuel a relationship for very long. The "other woman" can never permanently take a husband away from a wife by great sex alone. There has to be more. Usually what this woman has to offer, which the wife sometimes does not, is a keener interest in a man and a greater appreciation for his good qualities, things the wife may have taken for granted. The same is true, of course, where "another man" is involved with a straying wife. What I am suggesting is that the exotic sexual techniques recommended by some marriage manuals may seem fun and exciting but by themselves are never enough.

What Makes Great Sex Work

The real trick with sex is knowing how to keep the flame going once you have struck the match. As generations of happily married couples can attest, it is indeed possible to fine-tune the sexual aspect of the marriage so as to produce continuing moments of great joy. But you have to work at it. Like a beautiful new Mercedes Benz, you have to keep it tuned, oiled, and do the necessary maintenance and repairs. The same, of course, is true with all relationships.

What makes great sex really work is love, far more than technique. And mature love is *other*-centered. Sex must serve love, not vice versa.

Most men will stay with a woman they love even though the sex is not all that great. Fewer men will stay with a woman they do not love even if the sex is excellent.

Real love means loving your partner as is. Love is giving. Love is caring. Love doesn't keep score and may require the kind of sacrifice where you sometimes give but get nothing in return for a while. Good sex also requires good communication and feedback. Only then can you begin to explore your partner's sexuality, create a super high, and meet each of your deepest needs. But it cannot be done in ignorance.

The best sex is always part of a greater whole. It is a vital but interrelated part of a total relationship that draws nourishment from all other aspects of the marriage. This is a law of nature that never gets broken. Sex with a prostitute or someone you do not really know can never equal what is possible with someone you have a great and deeply committed relationship with, in trust, where total loving and giving occur.

Love also involves being responsible in the relationship. When David wiped out their joint bank account for some expensive power tools, it had an immediate impact on Alice's feelings of affection and sexual attraction toward him. When Jenny ridiculed George in front of company, it likewise affected his sexual feelings for her later that evening. He was remote and turned off.

To have a great, long-term sexual relationship with the one you love requires that you be friends, take care to constantly renew the romance, and make sacrifices. You must be responsible in your marital role and choose to forgive each other. You also need to know something about the nature of the psychological and biochemical functioning of sexual appetite and the unique needs of your partner. Knowledge is power. Thus right knowledge, focused energy, and commitment to your spouse may permit you to love superbly.

Also, remember that each time you have mutually satisfying sex in your marriage, you powerfully reinforce the pair-bond in your relationship, which enhances and encourages fidelity and trust. What is the moral? Frequent good sex cements and protects your marriage and overall relationship.

Ninety percent of great sex is in your head and your heart. Thus if you do not make the relationship work, eventually the sex will fizzle. This is why casual or recreational sex, where love is not a factor, often becomes boring. With repetition such sex becomes little more than mutual masturbation—empty and lonely. There is no real connection, no commitment, no real relationship to another human being.

How Men and Women Are Different

Men and women vary not only in their sexual anatomy but also in their biochemistry and subjective feelings about sex, as well as in many other ways. Each member of every pair has a different sexual history. They will always have somewhat varying values, expectations, and needs. Other gender differences include chromosomal structure; skeletal size and shape; menstruation and the capacity for pregnancy and lactation in females; greater constitutional vitality in females (they live longer); while men possess 50 percent greater brute strength and greater rate of basal metabolism. There are also striking differences in gland and hormone cycles and secretions, vital capacity, and average rate of heartbeat (eighty beats per minute for females versus seventy-two for males).

Consider the following facts about male sexuality as compared to females:

Men tend to be sexually aroused very quickly by visual, verbal, and tactual stimuli. They can also be quickly aroused to erection through recall of memories or thoughts of sexually exciting events. Thus most males beginning at about age thirteen experience sexual arousal.

Adolescent girls or even young adult single women are much less inclined to experience as strong an initial sexual appetite or get "turned on" as fully unless they have been sexually active with a partner for a period of time. Sometimes it may take a while (months or years) to "warm up." If perchance they have had highly negative sexual experiences or have been raised in a home with negative attitudes toward sex, they may never or only rarely experience sexual satisfaction, even though they might later bear five children or even marry five times.

It is very important for the husband to realize that even in a committed love relationship in marriage, a wife takes time to get ready for sex. She needs to be courted and prepared psychologically and physically. The husband may be ready for action in twenty or thirty seconds—but in most cases the wife is not. She usually needs to be prepared emotionally as well as physically.

The husband as skilled lover learns those individual things that cause his wife to respond and become receptive to his lovemaking. In fact, the best lover is the man who encourages his wife to communicate her needs and guide him in doing what pleases her most.

Frequency of Making Love—What's Normal?

In several decades of working with couples I have found that frequency of sex can vary from once a month to three times a day. If it is less than once a month, there is usually an age or illness problem *or* the couple is in the process of breaking up. One woman who visited me complained about having to make love to her husband three times a day. When he came home every noon it ruined her schedule. Twice a day was fine for her, but three times a day was asking just too much. They finally compromised on twice a day on weekdays and three times on Saturday and Sunday. Since the libidos of spouses will nearly always be at some variance, it means there must usually be some compromise in a loving, healthy marriage. If love motivates the relationship, this compromise can almost always be negotiated with understanding and consideration. However, when one partner's sexual drive is strongly inhibited or turned off, professional assistance may be required.

Pornography

Because of the serious problems it can bring to individuals, couples, and families, pornography of any kind should be avoided. It is primarily men, not women, who consume pornography. They use it for its arousal value, as well as out of curiosity. In my clinical practice I am finding increasing numbers of husbands, many otherwise devoutly religious, enmeshed in viewing this kind of material. Eventually such viewing leads to potential for addiction or dependence on pornography for sexual arousal and almost always, when it is discovered, disturbs the husband-wife relationship. Some husbands get to a point where they prefer this kind of fantasy sex rather than being intimate with their wives, and divorce is often the result.

With the men so involved, I find a common four-factor syndrome that tends to rule their lives: *addiction* (to the material viewed), *desensitization* (to the material's pathology), *escalation* (to rougher, more aberrant materials), and finally *acting out* (behaviorally imitating what they have witnessed in the porn consumed). This sometimes has led to a loss of church membership, to marital and family disruption, to divorce, and/or to many other unpleasant consequences.

Men and Women Perceive Sex Differently

Most women experience sex somewhat differently than men do. This is due to the differences in their anatomy, biochemistry, sexual history, and culturally conditioned roles. Differences in perceptions about the nature and meaning of sex can create occasional disharmony in the marital relationship for reasons that are nobody's fault.

Some wives whom I have seen in counseling feel that their husbands are sex maniacs. I sometimes hear, "The only thing he wants from me is sex. I'm just a body to him. I'm not a person. Any other woman could do the job just as well. I'm offended. I've become very turned off to him. The minute he is through with me sexually he's asleep and snoring. Yuk!"

The husband retorts grimly, "She's cold and unaffectionate. I need loving at least four or five times a week. She'll permit it only twice a month . . . maybe. I'm constantly furious and frustrated. I feel unwanted and unloved. I have a lot of anger toward her. All she cares about is that I give her the paycheck, keep her car running, and take care of the yard. In our bed most nights it's thirty degrees below zero. Yuk!"

Some women I see may feel guilty because they are not more sexual or up to their husband's level of need. Or sometimes the husband may feel chagrined or even apologetic because his sexual need is so much greater than his wife's. I have heard endless variations on this theme for countless years. It becomes in time a vicious circle. The cold and angry wife versus the rejected, sexually frustrated, and angry husband. This can sometimes set the stage for later infidelity or divorce. But with a new spouse in the next marriage, guess what happens? In a year or two the whole cycle often repeats itself. Once again a cold, upset wife and a frustrated, angry husband. Nothing really changes: same game, different players.

However, I must mention that in a minority of cases, I find the shoe is on the other foot. Approximately 25 percent of the wives I see tell me that their need for sexual intercourse is much greater than their husband's. "He's too tired, cold, or indifferent," they often complain. There is little doubt that some of the differences in husband and wife sexual appetites are based on genetics. Again, *nobody's fault!* So, the ideal sex frequency in any particular marriage will always represent some sort of compromise.

It's these differences and challenges that give life zest and permit us to grow, which, in the end, serves all of us.

Male Versus Female Sexual Focus

Mike and Joyce Grace, in their book *A Joyful Meeting—Sexuality and Marriage,* discuss the somewhat different perspectives men and women have about sexuality. With men the reproductive drive has an urgent focus on sex. Now!

However, as the Graces point out, with many females a major focus of their reproductive drive is on their nesting and maternal activities. There is an interest in intercourse as well, but it tends to be conditional on the husband filling his role as protector, provider, and co-parent. So if her husband isn't kind, a good friend, and helpful with the kids, she may just wear her chastity belt to bed that night, and her husband will find himself up a creek, and a cold one at that.

The Graces suggest that "men often have been judged animalistic and selfish because of the nature of their reproductive drive with its rather urgent focus on intercourse. On the other hand the female drive with its strong focus on the nest and children and less compelling focus on coitus has been interpreted as evidence that women are by nature more loving and more 'spiritual.' Or sometimes women have been labeled 'frigid' or 'not real women' because their attitudes towards sexual intercourse were not mirror images of their husbands'." Yet these differences are simply a reflection of biological and learned behavior peculiar to any man and woman.

A man often chooses a particular woman because of sexual attraction, which will always be a powerful part of his love for his wife.

A woman may also be attracted to her husband through a sexual or emotional chemistry, but in many cases, even more important will be her sense of deep rapport with him. Experiencing his sensitivity to her, his support, affection, and their mutual security in a special kind of intimacy can be irresistible to her. A woman can feel very affectionate toward her husband without any element of sexual desire. With males it is usually different. Affection and sexual desire are more nearly one.

The different ways the husband and wife perceive sex can create considerable confusion. The wife may wonder why Fred cannot be affectionate without always ending up with an erection and an intense need to have intercourse. She may think that Fred really doesn't love her. It is just his animal drive. Pure biology! Fred, on the other hand, interprets his wife's lack of sex interest as a lack of love and concern for him. It is very difficult for most men to be affectionate toward their wives without feeling some degree of sexual arousal at the same time.

Key to Male Self-Esteem

A major love need in most men is sexual acceptance. It is critical to a man's self-esteem, to valuing and accepting himself as a male, a father, and a husband. If he does not feel loved here, he will not feel loved at all. The loving wife helps her husband feel good about his male sexual nature, his virility, his organs, and his strong physical attraction and need for her. She is not afraid to caress or touch any part of his body or give herself completely to him in the act of physical love.

Some wives need to be reminded that sex is not a spectator sport. It requires participation by both parties. Having an active and exciting sexual life together reinforces the commitment of both partners.

Betsy, a minister's wife, had an excellent marriage. Despite that, her husband constantly complained to her about wanting more sex than he was getting. The quality was okay; it was just that he wasn't getting enough. With very active children and many civic and church responsibilities, she found her energy limited. Constant fatigue seemed to diminish her sexual desire.

One day she decided to do things differently. Starting Saturday morning she began seducing him three or four times a day. Whenever he showed up, she dragged him into the bedroom. Sunday morning he could barely drag himself to the pulpit to give his sermon. At the end of four days he was begging for relief. Totally exhausted and with glazed eyes, he found, to his surprise, that his insatiable appetite did have some limits. She reported, with a smile, that she has had no more complaints whatsoever about her supposed lack of bedroom desire.

Wives' Primary Love Need

I find that the primary love need of most wives is to be wanted, talked to, and accepted as a person—to be cherished, respected, and appreciated. And above all to be treated with kindness, consideration, and affection. *If the wife isn't loved in these areas and treated appropriately, she won't feel loved at all*—no matter how sexy or ardent her husband is later at night in his physical advances.

What I am suggesting is that in a great sexual relationship you give to get. But you give different things to get back different things. Your partner will have unique needs. Ask. Find out. Identify them and fill them.

In summary, sex should be a celebration. It comes from God. He created our sexual appetites and natures. He has ordained us to make love both physically and spiritually. He is pleased when He sees us bonded together sexually, in love, for this is the plan of creation. And this plan permits the husband and wife to jointly participate in creating new life and, in a sense, perpetuate part of themselves into eternity through their children. The sexual embrace should never be a chore or duty, but a loving part of a larger relationship; of giving to our partner; of cherishing, respecting, protecting each other. It won't always be easy. But the rewards can be incredibly great if we choose to make them so.

Twelve Keys to Joyful Sex

1. Be informed. Be a true expert on sex. Read whatever books or manuals you need on the topic. You would not

bake bread without a recipe. And this is much more important. Knowledge is power. However, be discriminating in what you read, taking care that you find material compatible with your values. Some of these books contain considerable misinformation—written by "quick-buck artists" rather than genuine experts and are essentially replacing old myths with new ones.

2. Make a commitment to yourself to have a good sexual relationship. And that means "showing up" for the event. Then give yourself permission! Love is a decision. Remember, sex is a gift from God to help bond husband and wife together and to allow them to participate in the creation of new life.

3. Be sure there is adequate preparation and foreplay—mentally and physically. This is especially necessary for the wife.

4. Have enough time. Don't rush it, savor it.

5. Have privacy (locks on the doors). No interruptions, no phones, no kids (get them to bed early or tell them you want some time alone).

6. Let things flow, let it happen, let it be fun. No agendas.

7. Establish and fiercely protect fidelity and trust in your relationship. With trust you feel secure, safe, protected, and loved. You can open up. You can let go. When trust is broken it can have a devastating effect on the sexual part of one's marital relationship.

8. Be positive with your partner. Build your spouse's self-image. Negatives and criticism kill sexual interest and appetite. People tend to become what we tell them they are! Lavish "positives" on them—continually!

9. Have a good relationship in other areas of your marriage. It's very difficult for an angry wife to get sexually aroused. Twenty minutes of focused attention at bedtime will not make up for eight previous hours of indifference or rudeness.

10. Mutual consent should be the rule in all that you do. Check things out with your spouse as you go. Nothing forced on an unwilling partner. Also, it is okay to cuddle affectionately and not always expect that sex *must* follow.

11. Open communication. Tell your partner what gives you pleasure and what doesn't as you caress and touch each other. Guide each other. Remember that most of us aren't mind readers. Be honest and open, but always in a considerate way.

12. Every month or so get away for a day or two at a romantic location. Break your daily routine. Even a weekend at a downtown hotel can breathe fresh air into your relationship and will not cost a fortune.

If you experience a persistent problem in your sexual relationship that defies your many attempts to remedy it, consult a competent, qualified counselor who shares your values. Check through friends, clergy, or your physician to find such a person who has special skills in this area.

All the really great marriages I know have a good quota of mutual affection. And an important part of this includes sexual loving.

CHAPTER 6

Pair-Bonding:
Renewing the Magic

What is the mysterious chemistry that so powerfully attracts one special man to one special woman? It is clearly a power of profound magnitude. It drives us to overcome all kinds of obstacles to be near the desired one, to overlook a multitude of obvious defects in our beloved. At times it looks like temporary insanity. Yet it is one of the most real forces in all of life.

However, the critical question is, How does one maintain it over time? How does one keep the chemistry working? Far too often it slips away as mysteriously as it appeared.

When two people, male and female, with different bodies, temperaments, cultural histories, values, egos, and neuroses are drawn together because of "the force," it's like an absurd contradiction, nature's practical joke. How can all of these differences result in attraction, harmony, commitment, love, and even sacrifice? It can only be termed a miracle, going back to the dim prehistoric creation period of man's and woman's bodies, intelligence, and spirit.

Ninety percent of all popular songs are about romance. And nearly all novels and short stories in one way or another involve love and romance and the emotional bonding of male with female.

Bonding

The bonding phenomenon gives us a special feeling of comfort, security, joy, and completeness when we are together and a kind of separation distress when we are apart.

I have found that bonding can occur swiftly and easily, or it can be a slow getting-acquainted process with many starts and halts, hesitations and uncertainties, but still arriving at the same ultimate destination. I've seen it happen both ways many times.

Another thing I keep rediscovering is that it takes more than a wedding to make a marriage. Even with great bonding you still have to continually nourish the relationship to make it permanent.

One spring afternoon several years ago I had dinner with a distinguished Houston psychiatrist. He was divorced. With him was a divorced social worker whom he was dating. As the conversation turned at one point to marriage and how to keep love alive, he commented that even a good therapist can have marital problems. He mentioned that his mother in Brooklyn had once given him some important advice on love and marriage, " 'Son, there are two things you must remember. First, you should marry the right person.' " Then the psychiatrist commented, "I forgot the second thing she said—but, you know, I did marry the right person. It was a great marriage. But I lost her. The second thing my mother told me came back to me many years later. 'Son, after you find that right person—then you have to make it work.' "

He concluded, "That I didn't do. My career came first. I neglected her. She felt too often abandoned and unloved. She left me. That was a divorce that should have never happened."

Nourishing Your Relationships

Love is always an ongoing process. You are never "there." It has to be constantly nourished in order to survive and thrive.

I have in my office a beautiful green plant given to me several years ago by one of my research assistants. It is very hardy and survives even with much neglect. Unfortunately, I am very forgetful about watering it. And sometimes it has to lose a few leaves and begin to shrivel up before I am shocked into action and give it water. In a way it symbolizes to me all marriages—including my own. Neglect is a one-way road to death in relationships. Every marriage—in fact, every friendship—has to be continually nourished in order to survive.

I see some couples who feel they can beat the odds by setting up housekeeping without benefit of judge or clergy. Their strategy, sometimes, is to see if they can make the relationship work, unmarried and without kids, before going to the altar. They want a money-back guarantee before saying, "I do." This is their way of avoiding divorce and making sure they are right for each other. But what they find in these common-law types of relationships is that they have to face the very same problems that married couples do. But since their arrangement is so much more tentative, with significantly less commitment, it is not surprising that the overwhelming majority do not survive. There are no legal or other types of support systems to help them stay together during times of stress.

Typically, after four or five failures in relationships like these, many retreat back into the singles' world bruised and confused, wondering why they can't ever make it in a relationship with a member of the opposite sex. As one young woman put it rather ruefully, "Now when I move in with a guy, I don't ask myself whether he will marry me, but only how long it'll last."

To protect themselves they feign an interest in their partner but never let themselves fall in love or commit themselves fully to that person. They hold back because when the breakup comes it'll just hurt that much more. Thus the cycle of approach and avoidance becomes highly repetitive and self-defeating.

Five Predictors of a Well-Bonded Marriage

Researcher J. R. Hines did an extensive study of two hundred married-couple relationships that worked—superbly. Dr. Hines found that there were five qualities that predicted successful long-term bonded marital relationships:

1. You like each other. There is a zing and excitement in being together.

2. You have shared interests. This allows you to be friends as well as lovers.

3. You have a reasonable agreement on the definition of male and female roles in your relationship.

4. You have similar values, goals, and philosophical or religious beliefs.

5. Your personalities and temperaments mesh reasonably well.

Four Key Skills

In addition to being reasonably compatible in the above five areas, Dr. Hines also found four kinds of special skills that were especially helpful in *sustaining* a good relationship:

1. A skill in meeting the other person's needs. In a sense you know how to "fill their cup."

2. A skill in communicating and negotiating so you can solve problems, make decisions, and work through conflicts successfully together.

3. A skill or competency in your marital role. This means, for example, being able to successfully earn a living, pay the bills, raise children, organize the house and keep it clean and attractive. Of course, marital roles are whatever you both define them to be and will vary from couple to couple.

4. A skill in adapting and adjusting in the areas of sex, finances, and personal habits (e.g., being clean, curbing temper, etc.).

One day in the University Counseling Center I met with Patty. She was an exceptionally attractive sorority girl. She was discussing Greg, a fraternity man whom she frequently dated. She lamented,

"He's a dream to date. He makes a girl feel marvelous, and on the dance floor he's the best I've ever been with. But I would never marry him." When I asked her why not, she indicated that he was a borderline alcoholic and his taste in women was strictly polygamous. Fidelity was an idea unknown to him. As a date he was great. But as a mate—no way!

And so it is with many people we associate with. We have to thoughtfully discriminate between those whose company we merely enjoy and others whom we also might trust our lives with in some kind of permanent relationship.

Again and again, I find, especially among women, a tendency among those with low self-esteem to fall in love with men who use and abuse them. The consequences are usually very unpleasant when the woman is later discarded. She may ultimately, in self-defense, even stop dating. Psychologists call this the approach-avoidance conflict.

Such people desperately want to be loved, to approach men (or women), but when they have been bruised enough times they become afraid to love, trust, approach, or try again. Essentially they are between a rock and a hard place. This can make people ill. I see a lot of them, and their most typical symptom is persisting depression. Individuals with this kind of history find it very difficult to bond to anybody. Fear of more hurt holds them back.

Can the Fire Be Rekindled?

But what about the people who are married and who once had a great romance, but the relationship is now sterile or sour? They and their spouse have become, in a sense, "married singles." Yes, there is a marriage license someplace. But they are married only in a legal sense now. The excitement, romance, and caring have long since gone. Most of the time there are cold silences. They endure maybe for the sake of the children, or maybe because of economic convenience, or because of the messy financial implications of divorce. There may even be perfunctory sex, but it is either a duty or a biological need, and not a real pleasure. Can such a couple rekindle the fire again?

In my experience, they can if they had it once before and the scar tissue of past trauma is not too great. But if they have never loved each other or the chemistry was never there to begin with, the prognosis is not very good. This doesn't mean they can't learn to live peacefully and amicably together. They can. But to experience romantic excitement on a continuing basis is probably not in the cards if it never existed in the beginning. You can't make a cake out of sand and gravel. You have to have the right ingredients to begin with.

Okay, the fire has gone out. How do we stoke it up again? How do we renew fun and excitement in our relationship? How do we rebond?

The "I Change First" Rule

Marriage counselor Richard Stuart, author of *Helping Couples Change*, has a great concept that applies here. He calls it the "I change first" rule. When a relationship or marriage sort of peters out, it is typical for each spouse to focus intensely on the other's inadequacies and failings. They become obsessed with them. With time their subtle or not so subtle put-downs make their partners increasingly supersensitive. The slightest intonation of voice is magnified in a highly negative way. Then each tends to sit back with cold anger and wait for the other to make the first move to reconcile. Too often this move never happens. Or if it does, it is so feeble that it offers no reinforcement. Or it comes too late. So they write each other off. At this stage of the relationship there is very little one can do to change a partner. *But everyone still has his or her free agency and can choose to change,* committing to love no matter what. What we are saying is that if *you* want to improve the relationship, *you must change first!*

Do an analysis of your relationship. What things does your partner want most from you? Then give it! And keep giving it! It will help heal the breach and soothe old wounds. At first your partner may be suspicious that strings are attached. Maybe it's only temporary. It's some kind of manipulation. But if you persist, the ice will melt. Your partner will usually thaw. Everybody, even the nastiest man in the world, wants love. No one can resist love given unconditionally, or at least not that I've ever seen.

The Fatal Error: Not Persisting

The mistake most people make in giving unconditional love is that they don't persist. I'm talking about months. If you want results instantly—*now*—forget it. Change, leading to rebonding, doesn't usually happen that way. If you make yourself lovable, it is noticed, and it will have impact and will make the relationship worth saving for your partner. You are nurturing your partner. And if there are problems with communication, schedule activities together that will improve your skills here.

Take a course in the evening; get therapy; take tennis, skiing, or racquetball instruction *as a couple.* Do whatever you need to do to break the vicious circle, the boredom, the staleness, and get yourself moving in the right direction. When good feelings are restored you can move ahead to negotiate the normal differences and challenges that face your everyday relationship.

In saying all of this, I am not suggesting that any woman should follow a man to hell (or vice versa), or that you can make a silk purse out of a sow's ear. When you go the extra mile to renew a tired, burned-out relationship, your partner still needs to possess some key good qualities that will make it all worthwhile. But what do you have to lose? The only places to go are out or up.

In summary, if you wish to rebond your relationship with your spouse, the following strategies will be helpful:

1. You first need to have a clear intention and commitment that you want this to happen.

2. Stop criticizing and correcting.

3. Launch a program of repeated affirmations wherein you give continuous positive feedback about the things that you like and approve of in your spouse.

4. Schedule private, relaxed, no-stress time together where you can renew your friendship, have fun, play together, have romance—in other words, think of it like courting all over again.

5. Be a good listener. Without interrupting, allow your spouse to get some hurts and negatives out in the open—this will be very healing. Don't defend yourself, just listen empathetically.

6. Finally, and most important—change your ways *first* and keep it up *no matter how unresponsive your spouse is at the outset*. No one can resist genuinely expressed love and attention. Good luck. Just try it.*

---

* You may want to consider securing cassette tapes which give positive strategies for helping your marriage relationship work better. Two cassette tapes by the author, Dr. Victor Cline, *Making a Good Marriage Great, Parts I and II* can be secured from Marriage Enrichment, 2087 Millstream Ln., Salt Lake City, Utah 84109 for $16.00.

CHAPTER 7

The Love Cycle:
Romance, Disillusionment, and Joy

There is a near universal and predictable cycle in love that has been true for most cultures and ages—for the early Romans, the later Elizabethans, our Puritan ancestors, the couples who currently live together unmarried, and, of course, for all the rest of us, too.

It usually starts during the courtship with a surge of romantic love that excites the senses and spirits to a heady euphoria. There is easy communication, incredible rapport, strong physical attraction, and a flow of warmth and goodness between the partners that makes them feel invincible. The mutual stroking seems to have no end. And the emotional bonding defies mortal intervention.

But always, as in the Cinderella story, sooner or later, the great carriage turns into a pumpkin or maybe an eight-year-old Chevy that's rusting through, and the beautiful princess becomes again what she has always really been—a mere scullery maid or maybe a clerk at J.C. Penney. And the young prince turns into Bucktooth Bowser, sometimes a little dull and often rather insensitive.

Thus with every love relationship, eventually the romance turns into disillusionment. This great denouement is dramatically and movingly highlighted during one of Marriage Encounter's special presentations. The wife discovers that her husband snores every night, is tight with money, and still expects to play ball several times a week with his unmarried male friends. *And* he watches too much TV.

On the other hand, the husband finds that his wife has a sharp, critical tongue, sometimes refuses to prepare his breakfast ("You leave too early—and besides I'm too tired"), and has lost much of the amorous passion that initially fueled their torrid romance.

Both pull back and before long become "married singles," ruefully trying to figure out what happened to their great love of the decade. Long, angry silences fill their nights together. And sometimes these become not so silent.

Most couples feel profoundly disappointed and cheated when they hit the disillusionment phase of their love cycle. They often are tempted to throw in the towel and find someone else. They think that if this is what marriage is all about, they want nothing to do with it. They may start having fantasies about old lovers or new prospects.

However, what most couples don't fully realize is that theirs is a universal experience in couple relationships and growth. They belong to a group that sooner or later all lovers join: The What Happened to Us? Club.

They are usually not aware—nobody told them—that it is possible, with considerable struggle, commitment, and effort to move through the "blahs" or disillusionment phase of their relationship into joy. This can really happen. Not only that, it can be better than even during the peak periods of one's courtship. I know because I've been there and have seen it happen to many other couples. I am not speaking here of ill-founded relationships that are acutely pathological and for which termination is the best and most merciful cure.

Despite this, too many couples incorrectly interpret the difficult part of their relationship as a sign that it won't and can't work. In some cases this may be true, but in most others it merely signifies that they (along with everyone else) have moved into the disillusionment phase of their relationship. But they needn't stay there.

When two people who are different biologically and emotionally, as men and women are, and who come from different family cultures bring all of this into an intimate relationship, they are going to get a lot of frustrating differences—and even pain. The meshing of two distinct personalities, no matter how much in love they are, will always involve at times some discomfort and stress.

Expect it. Plan for it. Don't be surprised by it. Welcome it as a chance for growth. It won't always be easy. But neither is writing a book, composing a symphony, running a twenty-six-mile marathon, getting an M.A. or Ph.D., winning a football game, raising good kids, or anything else worthwhile.

Some couples never leave disillusionment. I see their empty, drawn faces—hungry, unfed, and unloved. They get stalled there—eventually moving to divorce or enduring to the end as "married singles" in a sterile, distant relationship filled with conflict and disappointment. They keep a stiff upper lip. They may have occasional emotional involvements with others. But most of these are unsatisfying, and when they end they register in the psyche as still one more failure.

After a while a numbness and low-grade depression set in. These people may live out their lives through their children—but even this can be risky because their children may go through exactly the same cycle. When the kids' marriages fail, the grandparents (you) often end up in their old age raising the grandchildren.

The major thrust of this book is to tell you how to move from disillusionment into joy. How to move a solid marriage or even a shaky one to a new level of happiness.

Let me tell you my story. Our story. My wife, Lois, will join in, sharing some of herself with you.

When I first met Lois we were students at the University of California at Berkeley. These were calm, peaceful days, before the riots and demonstrations that would later hit the campus.

At that time I had no great interest in romance or marriage. I had a lot of tough school years ahead of me. Dating was for fun and laughs—nothing really serious. In fact, if I felt that there was any chance that I might really get serious with a girl or fall in love, I actually avoided her. I wanted to be in control. I didn't want anything like a serious emotional involvement interfering with the brutal competition of graduate school and getting my degree. I had seen too many other students fall by the wayside, rush into an early marriage and become burdened by the unexpected, un-wanted responsibilities of children and then under the resulting stress fail out of marriage and school. Not for me!

I had been raised in Los Angeles during the Depression. On our block my father was the only man employed. I saw people starving. I saw my mother take out food night after night to hungry families.

One night I overheard my father tell my mother that he was ashamed to let anyone know that he had a ten-dollar bill in his wallet. And then it was finally his turn, and I saw him unemployed for more than two years. I remember many nights when he would return from hunting for a job. The three of us children would anxiously inquire whether he had found any work today. We were scared. So was he.

I knew that I never wanted this to happen to me. When he finally did get a job—competing with more than a hundred applicants in a line—it was because he had some special technical skills that he had acquired during his time in college. I reasoned that education was one sure way of protecting me from job insecurity. And no woman was ever going to come between me and that goal.

LOIS: I was a freshman—really green when it came to graduate students. The first time I saw Victor was when he was giving a talk before a student group. I thought he looked somber and straight-laced. I wasn't too impressed until the next time I saw him when I had to pass off some requirements to join the student association. He was rather flirty, and I was flattered. He would flash a very cute smile at me. He was enthusiastic and fun. He had a great wit and kept us all laughing. I hadn't realized that he was the number-one eligible man whom everyone regarded as the "prize" until we were very noticeably attracted to each other. All during the semester I would sit in the library trying to study but couldn't concentrate and would just sit and think about him.

He was busy with his schoolwork, so we didn't see much of each other until the end of the school year and summer came. Summers he worked for the Southern Pacific Railroad as a dining-car steward. He had a run from Oakland to Ogden, Utah, that had him three days out and three days home. I could hardly wait through the three days he was gone. I lived for when his train would be back. This was the first time I'd ever felt this way about anybody. I felt buoyed up when I was with him. He made me feel like I was really somebody. He knew where he was going, and he made me feel secure. He was warm and loving and was interested in me as a person. He cared about me and my life.

VICTOR: When I first met Lois I was impressed with the happy smile that was always on her face. She was pleasant, warm, affectionate, not uptight. She was also flexible and reasonable. She was very comfortable. She had a special light in her eye that never went out. I instantly liked her. But I never, until much later, let her know how much. There never was any pressure or attempts on her part to control the situation or push me, which I had noticed in so many other girls and which always turned me off. She let me be me. She accepted me. But I played a cautious game. I didn't let her know how much I liked her. I wanted to keep all of my options open. I didn't want to get stuck with any premature commitments. In fact a good friend of mine asked her out for a date and suggested that I double with him, getting a date of my own. We went to a party-dance, and I found myself exchanging partners and spending more time dancing with Lois than with my own date.

The chemistry was great. She melted in my arms. There was a lot of joking and kidding. She could give as well as take in that lighthearted game of banter and repartee. And she wasn't intimidated by the fact that I was a second-year graduate student and she was a freshman.

She was a lot of fun. She was a person. And she had an extra dimension that deeply touched me. But I still wouldn't let her know completely how I felt. For a while it was still fun and games.

Watching, sensing how I felt, how she responded, I noticed that she never missed a cue. Intuitively she always did the right thing. Bold when she should be, but reticent and modest when it was appropriate. It was as if she had a sixth sense with her timing. And she had no hang-ups. She was never difficult.

This was a period of open exploration. Nothing was ever serious on the surface. But underneath was a constant searching, evaluating, probing, and asking, "Is she really as good as she appears? She seems terrific, but do my senses deceive me? Is she the real article?"

There were special moments when we'd turn off at the Berkeley pier late at night and across the dark bay see San Francisco like a towering emerald city lighting up the night sky. To the left was the soaring Bay Bridge connecting Oakland. And then to the right the Golden Gate Bridge. Small stardust lights traced their outline across the western sky. And sometimes all would be blotted out by the incoming coastal fog slowly creeping across the bay. As Lois nestled deep in my encircling arms we felt a unique closeness. There were long, effortless conversations, sometimes a comfortably secure silence. And the chemistry between us was always right.

LOIS: That fall when Victor returned to UC Berkeley, I entered a nursing school in Oakland. Somehow it all seemed unreal, like filling in until my real life was to begin. It was as though my real life was on the weekends when I would see Victor. Our dates were full of romance and excitement. When he'd bring me home it was torment to have to separate. I remember the first time he told me he loved me. It was one night when we were parked under a row of eucalyptus trees that were across the street from my home. He said, "I love you." And I couldn't believe my ears. So I thought I'd better wait until I heard it again before I exposed my feelings for him. It was a beautiful feeling to be able to open my heart up and let words express the love I felt for him. We became engaged, and because the nursing school did not allow their students to be married, I had to resign before we were able to marry.

VICTOR: When I first told Lois that I loved her, I was merely saying what we both knew and had deeply felt for a long time. The marriage proposal was not a surprise. It merely reaffirmed the very obvious fact that we really were right for each other.

LOIS: I obtained a job, and we made plans for a June wedding. Our honeymoon took us to Lake Tahoe and the national parks in southern Utah. It was a very natural step becoming Victor's wife.

We had some beautiful times in our little apartment adjacent to the Berkeley campus. I worked and he continued as a graduate student. How carefree it felt—just Victor and I as we attended plays and concerts in San Francisco and many social engagements with friends in the area.

What a wonderful and strange feeling it was when Victor got his doctorate and he was now Dr. Victor Cline. By this time I was expecting our first child. I couldn't have been happier. Very often I would walk over to the Life Sciences Building and look at the replicas that showed the growth and progress of the human embryo and fetus. It was fascinating. I had looked forward to being a wife and mother since I was a little girl. I remember as a young girl stuffing a pillow into my skirt to see what I'd look like when I was going to have a baby. And now, here I was, round and full of the kicking, thumping, living child of our union.

Vic's first job, as a research scientist, was down the California coast on the Monterey peninsula at Carmel. Those were three wonderful and fascinating years. We would often walk along the beach with the salt air blowing through our hair. Or we'd drive along the beautiful rugged shoreline, or hike on the rocks and search for seashells. My heart and life were now complete. It was a dream come true. This was the way we were.

VICTOR: Those first years of our marriage were golden. While there were the usual areas of adjustment that most newlyweds have to work through, Lois was a comfortable enough person and so very loving that these were easily taken in stride.

Our first real home was in Carmel. It was a little cottage nestled among the pine trees. Lois was by then quite far along in her pregnancy. I still remember with startling clarity the night when labor first started. We rushed her 120 miles to Oakland, which had the nearest hospital covered by our health insurance. Just in case we couldn't make it there in time I had every hospital between Carmel and the Bay Area plotted on my map. I knew where I could turn off if the baby were to come too soon.

A great storm swept northern California that night, drenching the coastal cities with torrents of rain. As I waited the long hours outside the Kaiser Hospital maternity room the thunder rippled

and crackled through the wet night air, as if ceremoniously herald-
ing the arrival of our firstborn. Then that magic moment arrived. I
was ushered to Lois's bedside. And there in her arms was a mag-
nificent baby boy. Tears of joy were on her face. She had achieved
one of the ultimate goals of her presence on this earth—to bring
forth a beautiful special spirit—conceived in love with a husband
who adored her very much. As our hands touched, our lips pressed
together, there was a special magic in that room. Never had I seen
Lois so soft, feminine, and fulfilled.

The years went by, and we found ourselves moving to Salt
Lake City, where I took a teaching position at the state university
as a young professor trying to get tenure and a promotion. It was
publish or perish. This meant doing a lot of research. Long hours,
six-day work weeks, and much night work, plus considerable travel.

LOIS: When we moved to this mountainous and beautiful state we
quickly found ourselves overscheduled and into myriad community and social activities. I became chief chauffeur, driving car-
pools of children to lessons, nursery school and the like.

Little things now seemed to irritate me about Vic that earlier
in our marriage I had thought were neat and sharp. When we were
dating I thought how great it was that Vic had such an intellectual
appetite. He was so bright. He had read so many books and knew
so much on such a variety of subjects. He was always up on the
international situation and the political scene. But as time went on,
his incessant reading, from the time he hit the front door, at the
dinner table, in the tub, in bed until who knew when, became very
irritating. Those one-sided conversations, with a programmed "uh-
huh" response, were very frustrating. And I'd get the same annoy-
ing "uh-huh" from him when he sat many hours watching football
on TV. I often felt very lonely, neglected, and disappointed. It was
almost as if we were living in two different worlds.

VICTOR: It was about this time that we had five preschoolers, with
three in diapers, including identical twins. Our washer and dryer
never stopped, day or night. And though we loved our children—
they were planned and wanted—the stresses in our respective
lives subtly and gradually separated us.

We went to bed tired. We got up tired—hardly knowing the other was there. Frequently we were "married singles."

The early excitement and romance in our courtship and marriage lost its glitter. We felt like jugglers trying to maintain twenty balls in the air at once, with all of our individual responsibilities. And occasionally something would be missed, and the balls would come clattering down. This often created ragged nerves, irritation, and disappointment with each other. Sometimes there would be long, frosty silences, sharp words, or tears. We knew we loved each other, but there was distance and frequent disappointment. To me it seemed as if the children always came first. Sometimes I felt neglected. Communication was often terse and critical during this period of disillusionment.

Why wasn't the laundry room cleaned up? Lois was upset because the faucet wasn't fixed and someone had forgot to put gas in the car last night—it ran out today on the freeway. I'd ask why dinner was always late. She'd retort, "Why can't we afford a car that will run—like our neighbors'?" "Why can't you spend more time with the children?" Lois then considered going to work. It seemed we were always short of money. I had no ready answers. I was spread so thin working as hard as I could to earn a living and trying to keep everybody happy.

LOIS: Our young family grew very rapidly to eight. And my feelings of being swallowed up by life grew along with them. At times I felt like I was being consumed by a voracious dragon. Every small problem loomed large and at times seemed insurmountable. It seemed that just as we thought of a way of tackling the needs of one child, another child's problem or special need would pop up in its place.

Up until then I had always felt like I could pretty well handle life's challenges all by myself—that I didn't need friends, a husband, or God. I was self-sufficient. I was thinking, "Who needs him—he's never around anyway. I'll just do my own thing, and he can do his."

But I felt an emptiness inside that shell of my being—a hunger for a deep relationship with God and Vic—as a friend, a companion, and confidant. I needed to feel loved, not just as a lover, but as a person. To be accepted on the merits of any likeable qualities which I might possess on my very own.

I started praying as well as reaching out to Vic with my needs. And one day he started to respond, unconditionally, with a greater love than I had ever before felt from him. I came to know the feeling with full trust and confidence that he would love and support me no matter what. God in His own quiet way reached out and blessed me.

Vic began, somehow, to make more time to share in decision making, upgrading our relations with the children and giving them more of himself. We also attended a Marriage Encounter and Marriage Enrichment weekend seminar. These events, taken all together, literally changed our lives completely. We haven't been quite the same since.

The little things that were irritating me before about Vic now seemed to dissolve. It no longer annoyed me to see the top of Vic's head over a book or magazine. I could accept him for the way he was and appreciate his good qualities.

Sure there are still stresses and differences at times. But our marriage is very different. We tasted some paradise—and we are not willing to settle for mediocrity or "bread crumbs" now. We went the full gamut—from a great romance into disillusionment and then to joy. And we have found that sometimes we can go through the whole cycle in even one day. But what we don't do is allow ourselves to stay disillusioned. We move out of it as quickly as we can when it occurs. We do it through our commitment to our marriage and our love for each other—and also because we know we have the power to change. *And so do you!*

CHAPTER 8

Personal Energy and Health:
Keeping in Shape

Low energy and poor health will always affect your marriage—no matter what else about it is good or right.

For one thing, it will put a damper on sex. It will also make you more vulnerable to depression. However, if your body is abounding with energy and is in top form, you will have a more positive, hopeful attitude. You will have the energy to face whatever problems and challenges confront you in your life together. Good health is a key factor in a sound marriage.

Fatigue and No Energy—How Come?

One morning a few years ago I woke up very tired. I had had a fairly good night's sleep. But the stress in my life was great. I just felt burned out. So I stayed in bed all day. I read a little and napped a lot. But in the evening I found that I still didn't feel really rested, just sluggish and indifferent. Even walking across the room was fatiguing.

My kids wanted to play with me, but my energy level was so low that I put them off. "Okay, okay—I'll play with you, but later!" Going out on the front lawn to retrieve the evening paper seemed like a major task. I asked someone else to get it.

Soon I began to dread getting up in the morning. On any pretext I would stay in bed as long as I could—just to catch up a little. I felt more tired getting up in the morning than when I went to bed the previous night.

Exhaustion and fatigue dominated my life for many months. My wife, Lois, would suggest that we do something, and I would amicably agree, but then when it came down to it, I would bail out and suggest that she go without me because on this particular night (which was really every night) I felt bushed.

Still No Solution

Typically, when I have a problem in my life I research it, checking all possible solutions, and try to do something about it. I tend to be a doer and a problem solver. As I read about the fatigue syndrome I thought it might be a nutritional deficiency: insufficient iron or hypoglycemia. My body might not be metabolizing sugar properly. So I upped my quota of vitamins and watched my diet. While things improved a little, my basic problem of low energy and fatigue hung on. Things didn't really change that much.

Again and again I read about the importance of daily exercise. So I decided that just as soon as I felt better and had a little more energy I would jog, swim, or do some other form of regular exercise. But for now I was just not up to it. The day never came. I always felt too weak and exhausted, despite otherwise reasonably good health. I had no other symptoms of a major illness. But the more I slept and rested the worse I felt. I also started feeling foggy mentally. I often found it hard to concentrate or remember things.

I regularly conduct psychological assessments on brain damage or elderly patients with mental slippage and know something about the physiology of the brain. I felt that I probably was not getting enough oxygen or glucose to all my neural tissues. Deep down I knew that I had to exercise if I were ever to get on top of things. Also, I got to the point where I was not functioning well as a father, husband, or even in my work assignments—something had to be done.

If I remained inactive and ate the wrong foods, my arteries would plug up and I would cut a number of years off my life. This life-or-death scenario finally pushed me over the exercise barrier. Since I did not inherit any of my ancestors' remarkable athletic abilities and am the gangling uncoordinated type, competitive sports were out—at least to begin with. So I started walking fast enough so that my pulse rate climbed into the aerobic range. I did this a minimum of twenty minutes a day, seven days a week. Then I gradually interspersed this with moderate jogging.

And a miracle occurred. The exercise didn't tire me out. It actually gave me more energy. I slept better. I felt fresher and sharper. My attitude changed; I felt more positive.

I also found that some of my symptoms were caused by allergies to certain foods (milk, corn, and wheat) as well as some substances in my environment. Avoiding the offending foods (for a time) and taking very mild medications which desensitized me to the irritants also helped.

Nutrition and Exercise: Vital Keys to Health

I am convinced that good nutrition and exercise are critical factors for good health. The food and chemicals that we take into our bodies daily have a profound influence, especially in the long haul, on our bodies' ability to resist disease and infection and perform all their complicated vital functions.

There is now a vast literature on nutrition and health, with new books coming out weekly. These are of variable quality, and I hesitate to recommend any particular one. Some are truly excellent. However, I would highly recommend two magazines that deal with these issues and report the latest information to a nonscientist audience in an understandable and highly readable way.

Prevention. (Emmaus, Pennsylvania 18098.) You can get a yearly subscription for $15.97.

Let's Live. (Box 74908, Los Angeles, California 90004.) For $19.95 (current rate at press time) you can get a year's subscription.

Both of these magazines originally tended to be excessively enthusiastic and overstate the virtues of the "natural way." Some of their early articles were based more on intuition and fads than on good scientific research. But I am happy to say that now the quality of the information and general accuracy in both magazines reflect the latest in scientific nutritional research. In addition, every issue of *Let's Live* contains reviews of recent new publications focusing on health and nutrition, which can be most helpful in finding those that might be appropriate for your special needs and interests.

Vitamins: Pro and Con

I am provitamin. I think they help. I also see them as an insurance policy. If your diet is by chance deficient in some essential vitamin or mineral, these supplements could help. When under great stress, in particular, you do not want your body deprived of any critical nutrient. I think we should protect ourselves. We have very little to lose by doing so.

I have heard (and read) some public health officials play down the usefulness of vitamins. But I would rather be safe. There is too much solid evidence demonstrating their value to disregard them. Scientists Lipton, Mailman, and Nemerof, for example, in a book titled *Nutrition and the Brain,* document the essential role of vitamins in normal brain functioning.

While vitamins can be purchased almost everywhere, including nearly every supermarket and drugstore in the country, I like to order through special mail-order houses because of their very competitive prices. Two of my favorites (which feature the natural over the synthetic products) are:

SDV Vitamins, Box 9215, Delray Beach, Florida 33482, and Lee Nutrition, 290 Main Street, Cambridge, Massachusetts 02142.

If you write to them they will send you their free catalogues listing all products and prices. I have no investment in either company and do not mean to imply that other reputable firms might not serve you just as well.

Six Preventable Contributors to Heart Attacks

Stanford University has a special heart-disease prevention program with various guidelines promoting a broad spectrum of good health practices. I will briefly summarize some of the main points of their program.

The Stanford program lists six key factors that contribute to heart attacks: (1) high blood cholesterol (due to improper diet); (2) high blood pressure; (3) cigarette smoking; (4) lack of exercise; (5) excess weight; and (6) stress. All of these are subject to our control—we can do something about them and reduce our risk not only of heart attacks but of a variety of other illnesses as well.

The program's findings clearly indicate that 80 to 90 percent of strokes and heart attacks can be prevented. First, you can eat to live—engage in "diet control." The Stanford researchers suggest that only 5 percent of us may require drugs to keep our blood cholesterol down—the rest of us can do this by moderating our intake of foods containing cholesterol and cutting out saturated fats. Salt and sugar should also be sharply reduced. The "good guy" foods are the complex carbohydrates: beans, vegetables, grains, and fresh fruits. Contrary to popular belief, a diet high in complex carbohydrates can actually help you lose weight. Thus potatoes, rice, corn, fish, low-fat cottage cheese, and legumes can all be consumed without guilt.

Exercise: How It Protects You

Exercise, as the Stanford researchers point out, is an *all-purpose* "risk reducer." It protects more than the heart. It improves circulation, generates greater energy, reduces tension, helps knock depression, and strengthens bones. However, these changes occur mainly through *aerobic* exercise, where you maintain a high pulse rate by brisk walking, jogging, cycling, swimming, cross-country skiing, and the like. Weight lifting and working out on most gym equipment will not do the trick. Only aerobic activity—a minimum of twenty minutes of activity without stopping, at least three times a week—can condition your cardiovascular system. I like to spend twenty or more minutes seven days a week. My best time is at the end of the day (after 10:00 P.M.) when everything else is finished. I have on occasion run in my basement, but it's more fun outside.

One formula the Stanford program suggests is to get your pulse rate up to 140 beats per minute if you are aged 20 to 29; 132 beats per minute if you are 30 to 39; 125 beats per minute if you are 40 to 49; and 115 per minute if you are 50 or older. If you have any special health or weight problems you should check with your physician about exercising. Before I learned about what it took to get my pulse up in the proper range, I used an electronic monitor with a clip to my ear that had a digital readout of my pulse rate while jogging. Once I learned what it took to get my pulse up in the proper range, I no longer needed it.

Being physically fit through exercise and good nutrition will definitely help you and your marriage because: (1) you'll have more energy; (2) you'll think clearer; (3) this is an antidote for stress, depression, and tension; (4) this will reduce fatigue, which inhibits sex; and (5) this will provide a positive continuing activity you can share with your spouse, which could include walking, bike riding, jogging, swimming, hiking, tennis, and so on.

The quality of your life and the quality of your marriage will be enhanced when you maintain good health. Your health should be an extremely high priority in your life. But you may just have to fight for it like I did. Good luck!

CHAPTER 9

Marriage Encounter and Marriage Enrichment: The Super Experience

I t caught my attention on a business trip to Los Angeles. I was in my hotel reading the *Los Angeles Times* and there it was—several pages devoted to coverage of Roman Catholics coming from all over the world to an International Marriage Encounter convention. Both text and pictures seemed remarkably enthusiastic, especially for the *Times*. Someone must be doing something right.

Even though I am not of that faith, as a longtime family counselor I had a curious interest in finding out what they were doing that would attract such an enormous gathering. Also, how were they able to generate so much enthusiasm among the normally skeptical reporters covering their convention? I cut the articles out and shared them with my wife upon my return home from Los Angeles. That may have been a mistake.

Two days later, and after several phone calls, she had us signed up to go to an "information night" and participate in their seminar. It was okay with them that we were not Catholics. Non-Catholics are graciously welcomed guests at Marriage Encounter weekends. For them it was a gift of love. There was no set price, even though we were given six meals each and a private motel room for the duration of the seminar. We could, if we chose, help defray expenses by later making an anonymous contribution of whatever we felt appropriate.

My private intention was to take a notebook and sit unobtrusively in the back of the seminar room—a conference room at the local Holiday Inn. I thought I might just pick up a few helpful ideas for my own counseling practice. I think that Lois was hoping for something more. I was so extremely busy in my life at that time, overextended and often away from home, that sometimes she wondered if she was really married, and if so to whom.

Very shortly after the seminar started I found that it was not quite what I had expected. This was not the typical professional meeting or workshop where one listened for two days to an expert with a blackboard and an overhead projector. I was pulled in as a very active participant. Lois and I soon found ourselves communicating with each other in a very personal and private way; we shared a number of powerful interpersonal experiences. In fact, at times I felt like a nonswimmer out in twelve feet of water. I was deeply challenged and profoundly moved by all that happened. In the end it turned out to be a powerful growth experience for us both. Our marriage has never been quite the same.

I would urge anyone to take advantage of these experiences. Couples who love each other and are committed to their marriage, though they still may be struggling with such things as communication problems, confusion about marital roles, disciplining kids, and anger outbursts, will find this a great treat, a marvelous valentine, and a real opportunity to renew the romance and joy of marriage. On the other hand, these seminars are not for couples with profoundly troubled marriages, though sometimes even highly divided husbands and wives derive great benefit—*if* they are willing to participate peacefully and open themselves up to the possibility for growth.

My wife and I, with other Latter-day Saint leader couples, have conducted similar seminars for eighteen years. Our emphasis is on improving marital communication and helping the couples to rebond with each other. This is done while always respecting a couple's personal privacy, and using approaches and procedures consistent with Latter-day Saint standards and values. It is nonprofit. Our time and labor are entirely donated, and we realize no financial gain. This we do as a gift to the community. The only costs are associated with renting hotel rooms, meeting space, meals, handouts, and office-clerical expenses, which are kept to an absolute minimum so as to make this experience more affordable to all interested couples.

Both International Marriage Encounter and a similar successful program called Marriage Enrichment give seminars in various parts of the United States as well as in many foreign countries.

Marriage Encounter is now available through most Protestant faiths, among Jews, as well as with the Catholics. There is usually a clergyman assisting in the presentations (rabbi, minister, or priest) along with lay leader couples. While reference is made to God, the religious aspects are not offensive or narrowly reflective of unique sectarian dogma. Thus members of other faiths and even agnostics are not particularly turned off by hearing that God wants our marriages to succeed. No attempts are made to convert anyone. The whole focus is on assisting the husband and wife renew their love for each other and improve their communication, self-awareness, and understanding of their partner's better self. This seminar is a celebration of the joy of marriage. And it really works. You can find out where these are given by contacting houses of worship in your community.

Marriage Enrichment has the same goals as Marriage Encounter but with no religious orientation.*

Costs are reasonable. These are nonprofit organizations. Leader couples are often drawn from the helping professions, but may be from other kinds of occupations and backgrounds. All couples are trained and certified before they are permitted to lead seminars.

If you want a safe, loving, super growth experience in your marriage, sign up. You'll never be quite the same again. And if you have gone once, go again. Our experience is that most couples

---

*You can obtain information by writing: Marriage Enrichment, 502 N. Broad Street, Box 10596, Winston-Salem, North Carolina 27101. Phone (910) 724-1526.

profit even more the second or third time around. This last point is extremely important. Because whether taking vitamins to improve your health or a shot of penicillin for a bad infection, one treatment alone almost never does the job. Good nutrition doesn't involve just one well-balanced meal. It's a continuous thing. Same with taking kids to church. They don't learn ethical and spiritual commitments from just one or two lessons from their Sunday-school teacher. We and they need to be *continually* nourished and invigorated in whatever area we wish to improve ourselves.

CHAPTER 10

The Extra Dimension

The "extra dimension" I'm talking about is God. Our Father in Heaven. Our Creator.

Taking advantage of His light and inspiration has made a difference in my marriage. And it can in yours if you choose to use this source of power, comfort, and direction.

Repeated public-opinion surveys have shown that nearly 96 percent of Americans believe in God. Four percent aren't sure. And only a small fraction of 1 percent are active atheists.

The reason belief in God is nearly universal, I would guess, is that in one way or another, at one time or another, most of us have had intimations of His presence and of His love and concern for us. We may doubt. We may struggle with our belief. We may never or only rarely attend a church or synagogue. But in the deepest recesses of our psyche we know that something exists out there, beyond us, but not far away. And it can have a dramatic impact on our lives.

A *Special Winter Day*

One winter day I was walking down the main concourse of the Behavior Science Building at the University of Utah where I teach and research. It was between classes and the halls were crowded with students. In the middle of this mass of confusion I was suddenly overcome with a terrible and penetrating anxiety. It focused clearly and powerfully on my eldest daughter, Janice, in her early twenties. I knew something terrible was happening or was about to happen to her, but I didn't have any idea what it was or where she was. And I felt totally helpless.

I tried to resist the feeling of apprehension that filled my whole being. It was ridiculous. Maybe I was just working too hard. It made no sense that I would feel like this in this crowded hallway at this time. I tried to reject this awful anxiety—but it got worse. I intuitively knew—absolutely—that something was wrong. Very wrong! So I prayed as I walked along, silently and with intensity.

"Wherever she is, please protect her! Watch over her! Be with her!" I pleaded earnestly and with such intensity that tears came to my eyes. I thought of all the missed opportunities when I could have spent more time with her, been a better father, provided more comfort and helpful counsel. I grieved that I had fallen short in being a better dad to her.

Then, as suddenly as it had come, the feeling left. I was at peace again. I went about my duties and continued my heavy work schedule.

About 6:40 P.M., while I was talking with someone in my seventh-floor office, my phone rang. I ordinarily don't answer it during conversations. But for some reason I did this time. It was Lois. "Honey—there's something I need to let you know about," I heard her familiar voice say.

I responded, "Could I call you back in a little bit—I'm in a conference right now."

"Well"—there was a pause—"this is something you probably want to know about right away. Janice had a terrible auto accident earlier today. She was heading up the mountain to the ski resort, and as she rounded a sharp curve she lost control of the car on a stretch of ice and snow. Her car slid headlong into the path of a huge truck coming toward her. The car is totally demolished."

Then Lois told me that another of our daughters, Robyn, had been with Janice. The force of the collision threw both girls against the windshield, and their bodies lay crumpled across the dashboard. The truck driver looking down at them in the torn wreckage was sure they were both dead.

My mind's eye saw that winding, steep mountain road—one of the very steepest grades in the country. In the winter it could be extremely treacherous. It had been the site of many bad—sometimes fatal—accidents. I remembered the times when, with cars stuck all over the road, I couldn't make it up the slippery slope, even with good snow tires, and had to turn the car around and inch slowly back down to safety in the valley below.

With a hesitating voice I asked if the girls were alive or injured. Lois assured me that although they had been temporarily stunned, they weren't injured. When I asked what time the accident had occurred Lois said, "Just a moment or so after two o'clock."

I was shocked. That was the exact time I'd felt that sudden anxiety. Just when she had needed it the most, I had said a fervent prayer on behalf of the very daughter who was driving the automobile.

Yes, I know that sometimes our loved ones die with no divine intervention. Still, something very special happened in this instance. I was warned. My prayer was heard. My daughters were protected and spared. Our family was blessed.

The Unwritten Agreement

My religious beliefs are very personal. And, frankly, I hesitate to share them. I work with many extraordinary talented and brilliant scientists who possess a great diversity of beliefs and nonbeliefs about religious matters. There is an unwritten agreement that we do not inflict our personal creeds upon each other. These are things that are beyond argument and persuasion.

Although this unwritten agreement allows peaceful working relationships among colleagues, it does not permit intimacy about some of the things that matter most in life.

Lois and I both believe in God. We are active in our faith. We have family and personal prayers. We say grace on our food before each meal. We pray for peace in the world, in our home, and in our marriage. And in a special way these daily prayers add an extra dimension to our relationship.

In blending our two unique personalities together, we experience the same joy—but also the same struggle, pain, and frustrations—that most couples experience even in the best of marriages. But something special is added when we have the assistance of God, the Father of our spirits, who created us as man and woman.

It's obvious to me that God is promarriage and profamily. He organized and created these institutions. He wants us to succeed in them. And I believe that if we knock and ask, He'll give us some help.

Our Free Agency Allows for Mistakes and Pain

To some degree, we all enjoy free agency. We have the power to choose. To do good or evil. To heal or injure. To behave wisely or foolishly. To overindulge our appetites or act in moderation. We each have the power to love or hate or be indifferent. We also can bring pain and sorrow into our own lives and into the lives of others—those who love and care about us, and those we care about. Freedom allows for the possibility of human error, sin, stupidity, and pain. But it also allows for growth, repentance, change, and renewal.

Sara and Larry—the Circle of Love

The most exciting events I witness as a clinical psychologist involve people changing, breaking destructive habits, shedding fear, and acquiring the courage to love, give, bless, and heal.

Larry wasn't living by the teachings of his church. He was an alcoholic. He wasn't very responsible. He wasn't much of a father to his three children—or much of a husband to his wife. But for reasons I didn't fully understand, his wife, Sara, hung in there. She didn't give up on him. But she pretty much raised the children alone. Her life was filled with stress, sorrow, and disappointment. But she possessed a quiet courage and faith for the future. She also knew her husband.

Although his heavy drinking frequently incapacitated him, she knew deep down he was a good man. Many women would have abandoned such a man or insisted that he shape up or ship out. Her intuition told her to stay—that eventually he would be healed and made whole. That is exactly what did happen through the love of two friends who reached out, touched his life, and helped him overcome his addiction to alcohol.

In the following years he became devoted to his church and his family. He frequently expressed extreme gratitude to his wife for not giving up on him. And he tried to make it up to her. They had many years of happiness together.

One day Sara's physician told her she had an incurable form of cancer. She had only a year, maybe two, to live. Those of us who had watched her care for Larry for so many years now witnessed his great love for her. He tenderly cared for her during her time of affliction and pain. He was now able to return to her a special love for her years of sacrifice in his behalf. The bread cast upon the waters came back to bless the giver.

I believe God can give us, as he gave Sara, inspiration and knowledge beyond our natural understanding. This inspiration can help us make decisions that have everything to do with our present and future happiness.

Solving Marital Problems—Getting Additional Help

As we struggle with challenges and problems in marriage, I believe it is important to use our own powers of reasoning and discernment as well as seek out good advice from others. Then as we struggle, let us ask God for additional help. God's help can come as a ray of light piercing through a gloomy fog. He can enlighten our minds with inspired strategies and solutions—with the correct path illuminated ahead. He can give us a deep sense of peace and certainty. The inspired solutions will have a harmony and rightness about them. We can then move forward without doubt and confusion, as if a giant boulder has been removed from the path before us.

I know there is a Father in Heaven who loves each one of us—even though we are imperfect. He loves us in the same way that we love our own children, even though they are not perfect either. I have seen this power at work in the lives of many people over many years. I cannot deny it. It is not an illusion. This faith represents one of the deepest and most important truths I know.

I also deeply sense that as Christ healed the lepers, made the blind see, and brought back Lazarus from the bonds of death, He can bless our disturbed relationships in marriage with a spiritual healing and renewal. He can release us from bitter memories and feelings, dissolving them and erasing them from our consciousness. The Holy One can profoundly transform our relationship and change our hearts through His grace and atonement. But I think we have to ask. Petition. It is a choice we must make in a lonely, personal way. It is between us and our Creator.

I believe marriage is sanctified and ordained by God as a way of meeting our most basic human and spiritual needs. I believe man is incomplete without the woman, and woman is incomplete without the man. The femaleness in the wife brings out the maleness in her husband, and the husband's maleness brings out the femininity in his wife. The resulting heightening of masculinity and femininity brings joy and zest to marriage. And as difficult and challenging as some male-female relationships can be, marriage still offers the most potential for growth and happiness.

Being alone as an adult is not natural or healthy, even though most of us will probably endure that condition for a period of time in our lives. But in most cases it will not be out of choice.

God will force nothing on us. We still have to choose Him—just as He has already chosen us—for the relationship to work. What I am suggesting is that we can communicate with God. Prayer works. And we can receive from Him inspiration and guidance as a freely given gift as we face the continuing problems and challenges common to all marriage and family relationships.

PART 2

Solutions for the Ten Most Common Problems Couples Face in Marriage Relationships

CHAPTER 11

Defusing Anger:
Handling Differences and Conflicts

It's okay to feel angry. To experience feelings honestly is what being human is all about. It makes us real. In fact, marriage counselor David Mace sees marital conflict as a "friend in disguise" because, if handled appropriately, it can lead to significant growth in the couple relationship.

A gentle carpenter, two thousand years ago, expressed anger in a Jerusalem temple when he observed moneychangers defiling that sacred place. Holy writ suggests that God, the role model for many of us, possesses emotional responses which include both love and anger.

The crucial issue with anger is how we handle it. This can be done responsibly so that differences are successfully reconciled, or destructively—in ways that ravage lives and destroy relationships.

Breakfast on the Rocks

Ted was built like a Neanderthal. His huge torso was flanked by powerful pistonlike arms. As he escorted his wife into the office, tears filled his eyes. Mary, on the other hand, was dry-eyed and composed. But her face was bruised, her right eye puffy.

When I asked how I could help, Mary nodded to Ted. This counseling business was his show.

He haltingly and with considerable emotion told me how they had been having breakfast alone together. The children were still asleep. As they ate and talked, Ted suddenly lunged across the table and struck his wife's face.

I asked Ted what Mary had done to provoke such a response. He sheepishly replied, "Well, it wasn't anything she said or did. I just didn't like that look on her face. So I lost my temper. I got angry—for no real reason, I guess."

There is plenty of research suggesting that *suppressing* anger is *not* dangerous to your health (you will not necessarily get an ulcer), while venting anger does not reduce it but actually makes it worse. Thus, lashing out at another person does not serve either of you. And it solves no problems. Visualizing lashing out does not help either and may actually aggravate the anger. Getting sympathy for your anger from a neighbor also makes it worse. However, talking it over with your partner makes it better. And solving the problem that led to the anger helps even more.

Psychologist Carol Tavris, author of *Anger: The Misunderstood Emotion*, concludes that "expressing anger makes you angrier, solidifies an angry attitude, and establishes a hostile habit."

A Universal Emotion

Anger is a universal emotion. It is a learned response to frustration, stress, and provocation. It can become a habit. We typically learn how to be angry from our parents. We see them pout; talk it through; verbally or physically abuse each other, us, or others; throw tantrums; become hostile and defiant; or rise above themselves to negotiate some sort of a peaceful solution.

Our response to the anger inside of us may be to become controlled and cold or maybe abusive and attacking. Some men take a "Sam the clam" approach and walk out of the house whenever an argument or difference arises. But this leaves the problem still unresolved, only to be faced again another day. On the other hand, the abusive shouting match is usually a lose-lose situation. It makes successful negotiation virtually impossible and can inflict deep wounds which leave the partners "married singles." It also wreaks havoc with affection and intimacy.

We have all experienced that flash of anger, the tremendous surge of violent feelings where we wanted to punch the boss in the nose, hit our spouse or one of the kids, or flush a neighbor kid down the toilet. Moisture may come to our eyes. Words may form in our throat—but remain unspoken—because of the certain instant dreadful consequences. We do not want to lose our job, divorce, or get charged by our neighbor with assault and battery. We hang on and discipline ourselves for a few brief moments. Then the ugly feeling is gone. We lick our wounds and go about our business. Thus, though we may briefly feel intense anger, it needn't be acted out. We can control its expression.

I find that the violent expression of anger is rarely necessary or therapeutic. It is usually, as mentioned, a habit learned early in life as a way of intimidating and manipulating other people. It is merely a technique for getting our way. Many husbands and wives I have seen have used this on each other as part of a power struggle, a way to get the upper hand.

Some people use the excuse of low blood sugar, alcohol, or premenstrual syndrome for their anger. It's not really my fault, they say. And it is certainly true that to some degree they might be more vulnerable and easily provoked. But I find that they can still control their anger if they choose, even though it may take extra effort.

Doris found that if she escalated her anger enough, she could usually get her way with George and the children. When she started screaming, breaking dishes, and punching, George would always play the role of peacemaker—which meant capitulating to her demands. Without fully realizing it George was reinforcing bad behavior and guaranteeing that his wife would again use the same angry and often violent behavior to intimidate and control. Abusive anger was strong medicine. It left even Doris feeling bad inside. But she kept using it because it worked. In time George both detested and somewhat feared his wife. He stayed in the marriage reluctantly, mainly to protect the children from her abuse.

Strategies for Anger Control

What do we do? Especially if it is true that differences and conflicts between couples are universal. And the same with anger. No two people will ever think alike or have identical needs, values, or goals. This is true for husbands and wives, parents and children, business partners, neighbors, and friends. So no matter how much a particular couple may love each other, they must either learn to negotiate their differences peacefully and reasonably or live in misery. In situations where one partner is powerful and dominating, it may mean the other is being exploited, which risks generating continuing hate, resentment, low self-esteem, and even depression in the "losing" partner.

On a number of occasions I have seen spouses who previously had expressed anger abusively toward their partner finally stop. But usually they did so only if they *had* to. As with any habit, such as smoking, if the doctor says you will die if you continue, you quit. But only when the consequences of continuing are too severe. It is not easy, but you still stop. Or remember a time when you were loudly arguing with your spouse and the phone rang. For forty seconds you carried on a warm, pleasant conversation. A few seconds later you returned to the battle. Of course anger can be turned off—if you wish. You do have control.

Edith was crying when I first met her. A few evenings before, her husband had told her he was getting out of the marriage. He had found someone else he loved and wanted to marry. He was leaving behind four children whom he had good relationships with. Noticing that she was very attractive, I asked why her husband would want to leave or get involved with someone else. Rather awkwardly she explained, "He doesn't like my temper. I constantly criticize and cut him down, he says. I'm always angry at him."

Then I asked her straight out, "Is it true?" "Yes, unfortunately, it's true. Too much of the time I'm angry and nasty. That's the way I was raised. I like to fight. And I do—a lot." There was a long pause, which I finally broke. "If you're going to keep him, I guess you are going to have to change." Guess what? Despite all the negative angry tapes in her head, she changed. She changed because she really wanted to. She chose to. And she had to—if she wanted him to stay around.

Seven Techniques to Keep Anger from Escalating

1. If you have a bad temper, the first step in handling it is to *briefly withdraw* from a high-risk situation before it explodes. Excuse yourself and go to the bathroom (stacked with magazines). Your family may hate you if you go out the front door, but the bathroom they may understand. And that is one place where they will leave you alone for a few moments. Come out when things are under control and you can rationally discuss the issue.

2. A technique in dealing with provocative anger-arousing remarks, if you are on the receiving end, is to *give back a soft answer.* Or *defuse the situation* by commenting, "You may have a point there," which is neither agreeing nor disagreeing with what others have just said. All it does is let them know that you heard them and are considering their point of view. It's a way of being neutral, keeping your options open, without admitting that they are right. A similar approach is *waiting till the person who has insulted you has calmed down,* then reasoning together thoughtfully. This really works. But you have to keep your cool, be patient, wait. It helps to practice or role-play this. It can be learned fairly easily.

3. Another approach is to *identify those cues that contribute to the anger.* After each conflict do a postmortem analysis, or psychological autopsy. Husbands, identify specifically what your wife does to provoke your outrage: does she call you a certain name? not make the bed? leave her hair dryer in the sink? write check overdrafts?

Wives, analyze what your husband does that triggers your wrath. It may be helpful to keep a behavioral diary of your anger experiences to analyze these incidents.

In this diary each spouse should record four items whenever he or she is angry: (1) circumstances surrounding the anger outburst (who was there, what led up to it, what triggered it?); (2) the specific behaviors occurring; (3) the reactions to those behaviors; and (4) the manner in which the conflict was eventually resolved.

Next, analyze these by yourself, then *with* your spouse. This amounts to a kind of consciousness raising. It makes you both extremely alert to what those anger-triggering acts or words might be, allowing you to have much greater control in stopping them in the future. Thus, the purpose of analyzing your anger diaries is to discover and interrupt the precise causes of anger, *not* just lay blame on either partner. Examples: a husband cracks his knuckles loudly, flirts, ignores his partner's requests, chews gum noisily, constantly jingles coins in his pocket, is overly critical of something his spouse does, belches frequently—which is highly irritating to the partner—and he keeps doing it. Or it could be that there are special moments of high stress or vulnerability for one or both spouses when they need some space, time to themselves without hassles, such as just after work or just before meals. Respect that time. Do whatever you have to do to keep the temperature in your relationship below boiling. You can choose to do this if you wish. It's not difficult at all. Just do it!

4. Another powerful device to defuse anger is *the appropriate use of humor.* Get everyone laughing. This can instantly turn a tense situation around. Henry Kissinger used humor with extraordinary skill when negotiating with the Arabs and Jews when he was secretary of state. Do the same in your home.

5. Still another effective approach is to *talk to yourself:* "As long as I keep my cool, I'm in control of the situation." "Easy does it! There's no point in getting mad." "It's okay if she's (he's) uptight. I can handle it."

6. Another "never fail" technique when discussing a very hot topic where feelings are high is to do it all via *writing letters* back and forth to each other. These should be written outside of each other's presence, then shared, read, and discussed together. Somehow, writing down both the problem and your feelings associated with it takes much of the sting

out of it. It becomes vastly more palatable to your partner. Try it and see. The letters, of course, should be written responsibly, not abusively. This is a very effective technique that frequently facilitates successful negotiation.

7. If your spouse has a violent temper and his or her rages sometimes escalate out of control, I would suggest that you *require*, as a condition for staying in the marriage, *attendance at a local anger control clinic.* These are usually sponsored by public agencies at moderate cost in most medium or larger cities in America. Inquire through your local social service people or women's support groups about the time and location of these facilities.

I have seen couples wherein the wife was raised in a home where fighting was the rule. Later in marriage she did not feel comfortable in a peaceful relationship with her husband, so she picked a fight with him every night. But this is like kicking a gentle dog. In time you can turn it into a snarly fighter, which is ultimately everyone's loss. Many, maybe most, spouses will not remain in such a destructive relationship.

In summary, the trick in handling anger is to "count to ten" and get past the initial flash point any way you can. Take a walk to another room, fake a coughing spell, feign a headache, excuse yourself to get a glass of water, go to the bathroom, and in any way possible interrupt the escalating anger. Identify the key triggers— words, behaviors, or ways you do things—which set off the anger response; then stop doing them. Use humor, and calm down by talking to yourself, give a soft answer, or disengage and leave, if necessary.

Thus, to reemphasize our main points: *Conflict and anger are universal and totally predictable ingredients in every marriage. This is not bad or wrong, any more than feeling hunger pains, fatigue, or a headache is. It is just a natural part of living. All these signs (anger or hunger, as examples) are merely signals suggesting to us to take some kind of corrective action.*

So, now that our anger has subsided, how do we best start negotiating through our differences? First you must be aware that the key goal of negotiation is not to see who is right or wrong, but to find a solution you both can live with.

I would recommend that you "score your wants" about any relevant disagreement.

Take a simple example. "How about a movie tonight?" "Frankly, I'd rather not. I'm a little too tired to really enjoy it." "Then, why don't we score it?" "Okay." "On a scale of zero to ten, how strongly do you feel about going?" "Oh, possibly, a five." "Well, I'm closer to a three. Maybe, since neither of us is that excited about going, we might postpone it a night or two. How is that with you?" "Fine. Let's try again Saturday night." "Okay. That sounds good."

By using this technique you clear the air. You know exactly where your partner is, and it makes the resolution of minor decisions much easier. It is a very helpful negotiating tool.

Three Ways to Negotiate a Difference

After scoring your wants, if further negotiation is necessary, there are three ways* to go in order to resolve a difference between the two of you.

"The gift of love." This amounts to acquiescence. You go along. You make a sacrifice. Because you love your partner and value the relationship you agree to go to the beach rather than the mountains for your vacation. You do something you may not particularly want to do because you care a great deal about making your relationship work. In a sense, the bottom line is that you give a gift of love to your partner without making a big fuss over it. But it is important that, on other occasions, your spouse likewise accommodate you. There must be reciprocity. It cannot always be a one-way street. But do not keep count of your sacrifices or gifts. That kills the spirit of the thing. Somehow the gift must come spontaneously from the heart.

One client, a woman of thirty, wanted very much to quit work and have a baby. The years were rolling on and they were still childless by choice. Her husband wanted to wait until they owned

---

(*Adapted from the writings of David Mace)

a home and had more savings. But their financial situation was un-changed from five years ago due to frequent winter ski trips, sum-mer cruises, and a live-it-up yuppie lifestyle. The husband finally agreed to support his wife in her desire to become pregnant be-cause, mainly, he wanted her to be happy. He gave a gift of love. But this has to go both ways. It is not healthy for just one partner to do all of the giving.

Compromise. In this instance, you meet somewhere in the middle in your negotiations. Both of you give some. It may not be exactly fifty-fifty. It could be forty-five–fifty-five, or even thirty-seventy. But here both partners give something so that both win.

Harry wanted to go fishing at Lake Powell next weekend while his wife indicated that a trip was long overdue to her folks, who lived two hundred and fifty miles away. After considerable discussion Jenny agreed to leave early Friday with Harry on his fishing trip. But they would leave the lake early Sunday morning and spend most of the rest of the day with her parents, who lived several hours from the lake. Through this compromise both parties were winners. It was a shared solution arrived at through peaceful negotiations.

Keep in mind that successful negotiations nearly always re-quire a climate of goodwill. And this comes from a history of nur-turing the relationship, a surplus of good times and good deeds.

If blocked, table the issue briefly. In some cases it's wise to table a problem we cannot resolve or a disagreement for which we cannot find a solution. In a sense we agree to disagree. We don't try to force a solution when one isn't available at this particular moment. What we are saying to each other is that it's okay for each of us to have different views on an issue or even have different goals. And this happens all of the time with people of goodwill who love each other very much. The important key here is not to demand an in-stant solution but rather allow for the passage of a little time, get new input on the problem, and look at it from new points of view. Then come back to the problem later when you are fresh and have new data. This approach makes differences much easier to resolve.

James had a good job offer out of state. His present employment was satisfying but did not pay as much. He wanted to resign, accept the new position, and move. His wife, Andrea, whose relatives lived nearby, had an excellent job. She did not want to move. It was too speculative and there were too many uncertainties.

She had heard many negative things about the city where they would be going. And she had major doubts that her husband could fit into the new position as he imagined he would. So she strongly resisted the move almost to the point of letting him know that if he left she would not come with him. Despite lengthy negotiations they could not come to any agreement on the issue. So they decided to delay the decision by three months while he would check other career opportunities and she would see if she might not find suitable employment in the city where her husband had hoped to move. The matter was quickly resolved six weeks later when James was offered a major advancement in his current employment, which included a very substantial salary boost and an opportunity to do some of the things he had dreamed of for many years. Of course, things do not always work out this conveniently. But, in my experience, giving an issue a little time to "cook on the back burner" is often likely to lead to a more positive outcome.

Ten Rules for Successful Conflict Resolution

At this point I'll briefly summarize some of the most successful approaches we know in negotiating differences between spouses:

1. *Choose a place where you will not be interrupted* by phone calls, door bells, or children wanting your attention. You may have a special "retreat" room in your home with a Do Not Interrupt sign, or you might both get in the car and park in the local school lot after closing hours. Or you might rent an inexpensive motel or hotel room once or twice a month as a hideaway where no one can get at you while you negotiate, plan, and love together.

2. *Have an agenda.* Be very specific. But always start your discussions with the brief easy topics. Save the real tough ones for the end. And when discussing a topic, stick with that one until you have decided what to do, even if you are required to carry the issue over to another meeting. Be

very careful about jumping all over the map in your discussions. Focus your energy on one issue at a time. This doesn't mean that you can't have fun or food as you do all of this. Make it as enjoyable as possible so your partner will look forward to spending that time alone with you again.

3. *No name-calling. No blaming.* No "It's all your fault." That gets you nowhere and just makes your partner more defensive and less willing to negotiate peacefully.

4. *No hitting sensitive spots.* "Hey, Fatty, I notice you're getting bald." Or "Where in the world did you get that dress—at a rummage sale?"

5. *Focus on the present and future.* The past is history. No garbage dumping! Focusing on past mistakes is like landing on flypaper! Concentrate on current and future issues. They are the ones that you can do something about.

6. *Be a good listener.* Don't interrupt! Let your partner have a full say, then ask for elaboration or explanation, as necessary. Repeat back (feedback) in a brief summary what you thought your partner said and ask for confirmation. "Is that what you said?"

7. Avoid the *"My way or else!"* trap, or the "I have to win at any cost" approach. Look for new solutions and new alternatives that allow both of you to win. This may require some preplanning on your part. Come up with two or three alternatives. Which does your partner like best?

8. If your discussion becomes heated, *hold hands.* Face each other while you talk, clasping both hands together. And *do not let go* until you have had some progress on the issue being discussed. When you hold hands it is a way of saying "I still care, you are very important to me"—even though you may not agree on everything. It also keeps you responsible. You cannot run away. Most couples end up

laughing together when they do this. Its effect is magic. And I'm not quite sure why.

9. Finish the discussion and *write down your agreements*, even if it's only to table the matter and return to it later.

10. A final approach is sometimes called *the "triangle."* Think of husband and wife facing each other at the bottom two legs (or corners) of a triangle, attempting to resolve a problem or difference which each has strong opposing views about. In many instances it is an ego thing, or "I'm right. I want to do it my way—not yours!" And there may be considerable headknocking and jousting, each trying to get his or her way.

If you imagine God at the apex of your triangle and your marriage, and each turn to Him and ask, "What is Thy will?" and then together pray about the matter—it has the potential of totally changing things around. And as you approach God, seeking His direction, you both come closer together spiritually as the two legs of the triangle approach the apex, or God. Thus the solution is no longer an issue of which one of you wins in this contest but a matter of each of you choosing to submit to His will and inspiration.

And a final bonus suggestion: Look for the positive message or intent in what your partner is saying. If the husband asked, "Can I help you clean the house this morning?" this could be viewed by the wife as, "He's criticizing me! He must think I'm a dirty housekeeper," or "Hey! that's great. He wants to help out. What a loving husband!" Look for the *positive intent* when listening to what your spouse has to say.

Express Appreciation

Then when you are finished, *express appreciation to your partner for being there and contributing to making your relationship better. Express positives that reflect the good that you see in them.* You can never do too much of that. It is like magic to the ears. We all need it.

Remember, in successful conflict resolution the real goal is *equity*. A fair share for each. A fair share of the rewards as well as the chores. In a power struggle with your mate, winning can be losing! You always want both of you to come away from the table with something. Compromise is definitely better than getting everything your own way. Give to get.

Also remember to use "I" messages, not "You" messages. Speak for yourself. "You are . . ." messages are nearly always judgmental and accusatory. They often involve garbage dumping. They do not solve problems, they create them.

Let me conclude this chapter with an "I" message, the three most important words in the English language: *I love you*. Let those you care about hear it often.

CHAPTER 12

The Immature Partner:
Lazy, Irresponsible, and Selfish

Ifit were not for the twins, Alicia would have left Fred long ago.
But it turned out to be just her luck—pregnant on the honeymoon.
She had hoped to finish school before ever starting a family.

To Alicia, Fred was a nerd, an oaf—impossibly demanding,
selfish to the core, hopelessly boyish. But that was what originally
made him seem so attractive to her. That innocence, that impish-
ness, those big eyes, so surprised and guileless when she caught
him in the act of doing a hundred things he had no right to do without checking with her. What about common courtesy? Decency?
Did he know what those meant? Where was his mother when he
was growing up? She wondered sometimes if he ever really had a
mother. Perhaps they found him out in a field somewhere.

Typically, immature people are annoyingly selfish and irresponsible; they break commitments, demand their own way, have frequent
pouting spells or temper tantrums, are undependable, and do not follow through—and they do not seem to be aware of the consequences
of their behavior. They are a pain to deal with. And yet at the same
time they can be fun, attractive, sexy, the life of the party, and sometimes very affectionate and giving. Still, what to do with them?

Often the other partner has to assume an almost parental role, do what the original parents failed to do: teach responsibility and civility, and encourage growing up.

Too-Eager Jenny

Jenny was a tall, thin girl who matured late. She did not date through most of her teen years because, as she tearfully put it, "I just looked like a lamp post." But eventually the day came when her pituitary and gonadotrophic glands fired up and she blossomed into a strikingly beautiful young woman who caught the eyes of many young men.

She said yes to the first proposal when she was barely eighteen and left for a blissful honeymoon with a man many years older. He had swept her off her feet with charm and sophistication. However, he had a history of being unable to hold a job for more than a few weeks. And being married did not change this pattern. He was soon out of work again, and she, to help out, began working in a fast-food restaurant at minimum wage. He somehow was never able to find a job again, so she supported him. While he was pleasant and seemed appreciative, he only dreamed (but never did anything) about sometime making it big. Someday he would make lots of money; then he would buy her beautiful clothes, a nice new car—anything she wanted. Three babies later she found him disappearing for weeks—he was out looking for a job in some other city where the "opportunities were much better." He would return at unexpected times urgently in need of sex and food. One year she finally got the message. He was not going to change for her or anyone else. His promises and grandiose plans for the future were empty and meaningless. She finally ended the relationship.

Cornflakes and No Milk

Jerry was in his second year of law school when he married Sally, a very sexy bit of feminine fluff. He had met her on a blind date. She came from a well-known family with established social connections. Within hours after their three-day honeymoon he found that she knew nothing about food preparation, apartment cleaning, handling money, or relationships. He married her mainly because of a very strong sexual chemistry between the two.

His first breakfast consisted of cornflakes and an apology for no milk. The second morning she complained of a headache and asked him to get his own breakfast. Dinners were frozen or eaten out.

Her main source of stimulation while he was at the university was soap operas or long phone conversations with friends. She refused to go to work because she felt it was the man's position to support the wife. She had quit college after getting married and with some relief: too many low grades caused mainly by poor study habits and scattered interests.

For years she had gotten by on her cuteness, full figure, and charm. Being an only daughter, she had been indulged and pampered by doting parents who had made most of her decisions for her. She found herself calling her mother constantly on the phone about the most trivial matters as well as what to do about the frequent upsets she had with her husband. She complained because he spent many evenings studying rather than doing things with her. She felt very irritated by their lack of money. Eventually her husband suggested that they get counseling at the university guidance center. She agreed and the outcome eighteen months later was very positive. She made some adjustments, got an interesting part-time job, took an evening class, and did a lot of maturing. They stayed together.

The Retreads Who Made It

Linda and Frank made a great pair. They had raised four kids, and they were having a ball. In their middle fifties they were what I regarded as a beautifully matched couple. It was clearly a great marriage. They had a lot of joy and companionship together.

When I asked Linda how long they had been married she said, "Thirty-three years . . . well not exactly." She looked a little flustered. Frank, with a grin on his face helped her out. "Well, it's like this. We were married twice. Our first marriage lasted a year. We were just immature kids. We couldn't handle the responsibility of married life. We were just too young. Three years later we married each other again, and it worked."

It was very clear that during their three years unmarried and apart they each gained more mature attitudes and skills in making relationships work. They have a superbly happy marriage now. The things they learned during those three years (in addition to being turned off by the singles' scene) had to do with commitment, flexibility, handling stress, and especially communication and negotiating with courtesy and common sense.

I do not think a three-year divorce is the ideal solution for a marriage that is handicapped by immaturity. In most instances, couples can work things out in their present marriage. But it won't be easy and will require much time and patience as well as a long-term commitment to the relationship.

Ten Strategies for Dealing with an Immature Spouse

1. You first must clearly decide whether both of you want to stay in the marriage and work things out. Change is painful. Working things out between you will not be easy. But you both must have a clear intention that you want the marriage to work.

2. You next need to clearly identify which immature behaviors in your partner are most objectionable to you. This needs to be done for *both* husband and wife. It is most important that these be written down.

3. From this list, each of you choose the specific behavior that you would most like to see changed. It is critical that this be something clear, behavioral, and definable, and that it can indeed be changed. Good examples might be "[name] will keep a record of all checks written, with current balance entered" or "[name] will not call partner obscene names during times when they disagree." Poor examples would be "treat spouse better," or "don't be so mean," or "spend money more wisely." These are too vague.

4. Work on only one behavior at a time. Focus all of your energy in changing or modifying that one. Don't try to

change everything at once. It will never work. Then get feedback from your mate on how you are doing. When one problem behavior changes or eases up, then move to the next one. Some couples will be able to do all of this by themselves. Others will require the help of a counselor for motivation and to check on compliance. I find that it sometimes helps greatly to have a neutral third party, such as the counselor whom we have to be responsible to, who'll keep us on our toes and give us helpful suggestions and feedback on how we're doing.

5. Do not expect perfection. Behavior changes occur gradually, never all at once. If the husband uses bad language in front of the kids, reducing it from five times to once a week is a victory, not a failure, for him. What you are interested in is the *direction* in which he is going with his problem, not whether it is instantly mastered. And of course the same is true for you and your problem behaviors.

6. You should next aim for changes in spirit and attitude. You want some joy in your partnership. This is something that you can never force singlehandedly. But you can do a lot to create good feelings between the two of you. Offer lots of positive reinforcement. Let your spouse know when he or she does something you appreciate. Use humor whenever you can to lighten difficult situations. Don't be so serious. Make sure that you are doing some fun things together. What did you do together during your courtship that was fun? Roller skating, visiting with friends, dancing, boating, hiking, soaking in the hot tub at the spa? Revive it.

7. Whatever your program or goals for behavior change, *don't give up too soon*. Keep it up. Even if it appears not to be working as quickly as you wish. Change can definitely occur. But you do have to be patient.

8. Have some interests beyond your relationship with your spouse. No matter how wonderful she may be, she will never be able to meet all of your needs, just as you can never meet all of hers. Thus, it is important to cultivate a network of good friends, special interests, hobbies, sports, and friendly relatives who can also help fill your cup. Most of these may be shared with your spouse, but some won't. He may like fishing, but you don't. Or you are the jogger, and she isn't. That's okay. In doing this it must be extremely clear to all that your highest priority is always your marriage. But in order to have balance and joy in your life, you need food from many sources. No marriage can provide everything you need. Encourage and support a similar balance in the life of your spouse. He'll then be able to give more back to you because his cup is full.

9. If your spouse suffers from poor judgment, in my experience this usually doesn't change much over time. The question is, can you live with it—considering everything? Can you take a balancing, compensating role? Will he or has he permitted this in the past?

10. Join a co-dependency support group. They are free. They meet weekly and exist in nearly every community in the United States. Check out several to find the one that is the best fit for you. Their purpose is to help you deal with awkward, difficult relationships. Each community usually has a clearinghouse that lists most of these groups plus when and where they meet. You may have to do some calling around on your phone to tap into this network. I belong to one. I think they are great.

CHAPTER 13

Surviving with a
Jealous Spouse

The Nature of the Beast

Being married to a jealous spouse can be an extremely trying experience. Initially you might feel a little flattered by a partner "caring" that much about you. But as time goes on, it becomes obvious that it is a selfish, possessive caring and soon becomes like a pebble in your shoe—increasingly irritating. It may in time disturb or even destroy love and desire for the partner. And to the suspicious lover, jealousy is hell, a jaundice of the soul, a self-defined torment. As one husband put it, "My jealousy is like an obsession—it consumes me day and night. At times I want to kill my wife, then those whom I see as my rivals, then finally myself. I hate it. I hate the way I am. But I still can't get rid of it."

Jealousy can show up in other ways, such as perceiving that others are favored over you; or interpreting nearly anything a partner may say or do as proof that she is not on your side or is against you; or being envious or resentful of others' possessions, position, or circumstances.

Jealousy is often irrational; you cannot argue with it. It can be obsessive, all-consuming. In an extreme form it can be a sickness—full of envy, resentment, anger, suspicion, and anxiety. Because of its power and prevalence, it is a common theme in literature: Adam's son Cain killed his brother Abel because of it; Othello killed his bride, Desdemona, in a jealous rage. When consumed by jealousy we cannot feel love. Knowing why does not help. Just trying to will it away will not cure it. However, in some rare instances it can be one of many signs suggesting the presence of a more serious personality disturbance (or even more rarely a psychotic type of illness).

Domestic Violence and Jealousy

A large number of instances of domestic violence are occasioned by a jealous spouse or ex-spouse inflicting retribution on what they perceive to be an erring partner. Consider the O.J. Simpson case widely covered by the media. Whether you believe Mr. Simpson was or wasn't guilty of homicide, there is much direct evidence of his inordinate jealousy and repeated physical and verbal abuse of his ex-wife, Nicole, for her rejecting him and being with other men.

In a recent *Psychology Today* survey of twenty-five thousand of its readers, representing a fairly sophisticated sample of Americans, 98 percent saw monogamy (sexual exclusiveness) as important for them in their marriage or committed relationship. Virtually nobody wants to be deceived or cheated on—even in this modern liberated age. If you disturb that trust bond, you will awaken dark forces in your partner.

Origins of Jealous Feelings

In many cases the roots of jealousy are related to unresolved early childhood attachments. This may have involved rejection, abandonment, or preference of other siblings by parents or other key people in a person's life. At its core the three key emotions involved in jealousy are loss of self-esteem, grief, and hatred.

Jealousy can also stem from a fear of the loss of a loved one to some rival. Usually the jealous person has some feelings of insecurity, less power in the relationship, or low self-esteem to begin with. He is more vulnerable and easily threatened. He may become quite paranoid about any innocent contact his partner has with another person. He may accuse her, often unrightfully, of infidelity, perfidy, or disloyalty in action or intent. He may cross-examine his spouse for hours on where she has been or who she has talked to. He may attempt, in an outrageous way, to limit where his spouse goes or who her friends might be. It can become very suffocating.

Sometimes, however, the jealous spouse may be *projecting* his own lustful desires or interest in others onto his innocent spouse. He assumes (nearly always incorrectly) that his partner must have the very same temptation to stray that he does. And this makes him very suspicious and angry.

Hank's Story

Hank's first wife repeatedly cheated on him. He had loved her very dearly, and each new discovery of infidelity caused immeasurable pain. To make things worse, his parents had behaved somewhat the same way. He had witnessed that sadness firsthand while growing up.

When, with great hesitation but also courage, he went into his second marriage, he found himself obsessively distrustful and anxious of every contact his wife, Linda, had with other men. He would routinely interrogate her every night about everything she had done that day. He knew this behavior upset his new bride, but he just could not help it. He was totally possessed with jealous anxiety. He was haunted by thoughts that she just might find somebody else she would like better. At root it was a fear of abandonment by someone he loved and needed.

While we can sympathize with Hank's situation and understand the origins of his jealous behavior, we can also see why he will not be an easy person to live with. Linda will, with time, become ever more miserable being constantly under his surveillance. It will be increasingly difficult for her to feel warm and tender toward her distrusting husband. In a sense she is being continually punished for his first wife's and his parents' mistakes. As time passes, Linda will probably feel increasingly put-upon and misunderstood, and Hank by his suspiciousness may actually provoke the very thing he fears the most—her leaving him for someone else.

Jealous Matt

Matt, a successful engineer, suspected that his wife was having lustful thoughts whenever she looked at another male in his presence. In order to keep peace with her husband, it became necessary for her to bow her head and stare at the sidewalk as they walked down the street together or at the floor if they were inside at a social gathering. It was at this point that she decided to get help and see a counselor.

Three Types of Marital Jealousy

Let's review several types of marital jealousy:

1. An appropriate or legitimate *reality-based concern* or "jealousy." This occurs where one's spouse has a history of breaking her marital vows through inappropriate relationships or loyalties outside the marriage. The trust bond in the marriage has been repeatedly broken. The pain, doubt, and distrust felt for the partner has a genuine basis in fact. The truth is—your spouse is not honoring her marriage vows, is deceitful, and is playing fast and loose with outside romantic involvements. Whether divorce is the answer or whether a reconciliation and healing are possible will be determined by the motivations and interest of each spouse and how they choose together to negotiate about what's happened.

2. The second type of jealous spouse has a *paranoid personality disorder*—a form of mental or emotional illness. While disruptive at times, these people can usually hold jobs and function reasonably well in most other aspects of everyday life. This illness can be mild, moderate, or severe in nature.

It is twice as prevalent in men as women. There is some evidence that this can have genetic as well as environmental or "family of origin" contributors.

One partner, as an example, may be insanely jealous of any contact, no matter how appropriate, that the other has with members of the opposite or even same sex. This, in part, may be due to a character illness he has that won't go away. He makes an awful pest of himself. He frequently questions without justification the loyalty, fidelity, or trustworthiness of his spouse. In short—he is paranoid in some of his thinking. He uses the defense of projection; that is, he attributes to others and accuses them of impulses and thoughts that he is unable to accept in himself. He prides himself on being rational and objective, but such is not the case. This may require focused counseling and even medication to heal and save the marriage.

3. *Psychotic illness.* Occasionally a spouse may have a rare but much more serious mental illness, such as early stages of schizophrenia (paranoid type) in which she may be delusional and falsely accuse her partner of infidelity or other misdeeds. She may hallucinate or think or see and believe things that are not real. She is much out of contact with reality, imagining behaviors that are totally unreal and absurd. On occasion she can be dangerous. If this is the problem, the loss of contact with reality will usually show up in a number of other ways also. She will generally act strangely. This is a major mental illness. Such people will probably require medication and treatment by a physician or psychiatrist. Talk therapy by itself, "turning the other cheek," trying to reason with them, or just forgiving them for what they have done won't change anything. They are mentally ill and usually exhibit confused, illogical thinking. This won't change unless given special medical assistance.

When I first see a couple with a jealous spouse problem, for me the key question or issue is, is there any valid reason for one or both spouses to be jealous? Has there been a history of rejection or abandonment by one partner, or flirtations or affairs with others by the other partner? Or is this jealousy an illogical, obsessive illness or condition that has no justified basis?

Sometimes a spouse has good reason to be jealous. Perhaps his mate has sown the seeds of anxious concern by flirting or becoming too intimate with a third party. In some situations, this can be like opening Pandora's box. Once you break the trust bond in your relationship by having an inappropriate involvement with other persons, you awaken a monster that can create an enormous amount of distrust, doubt, suspicion, and pain. This poisons the relationship and creates much mischief in the marriage.

My case files are full of sad stories documenting this, with many marriages finally ending in divorce. However, it is most important to emphasize the difference between a *justified*, reality-based jealous concern (plain old common sense) when one partner has a history of "playing around" and an unfounded, irrational jealousy occasioned by a partner's appropriate nonintimate relations with others. There is a big difference!

The solution to jealousy in the former instance must be a change of behavior by the unfaithful spouse: stop cheating or you will reap the whirlwind! Appropriate confrontation, with proof, will usually be required as the first step in healing; perhaps a brief separation may be necessary. To make accusations without verification or good evidence is very risky business. A guilty spouse can deny and lie and make her mate look foolish. Then she is not held accountable and nothing changes.

Some Solutions

The appropriate solution depends on which type of jealousy we are dealing with. If a partner is repeatedly unfaithful or engaging in inappropriate liaisons with third parties, this must stop. You will have to confront your spouse. You cannot look the other way indefinitely. Such inappropriate behaviors will always disturb any marital relationship as long as they continue.

Compulsive promiscuity outside of one's marriage can be a consuming illness, maybe an addiction. I treat many with this problem. Promises to reform or do better rarely work because, like an alcoholic, they lose the power to control their behavior or say no to temptation. Each revealed or discovered indiscretion represents another trauma to the other spouse and another step towards divorce. This is a treatable problem, but the erring partner must be challenged and willing or motivated to get help.

If your partner has a paranoid personality disorder—he will need professional help to overcome the problem. If he is left untreated, the unjustified accusations and jealous storms will continue to sorely stress the marriage. Gentle counseling combined with appropriate antianxiety medication and small dosages of antipsychotic drugs (such as Mellaril or Haldol) for brief periods can be helpful.

With a psychotic illness (schizophrenia), appropriate antipsychotic medications given long term plus personal talking therapy are often very useful in bringing about change and healing.

There are also other types of jealousy disorders involving immaturity, selfishness, a need to control a marital partner, or acutely dysfunctional home backgrounds. Each spouse will need wise strategies to soften and ameliorate their impact on the marriage. Seeking out competent professional care may make a major difference in dealing with it. Good luck.

CHAPTER 14

Coping with Violence

I am in my thirties and so is my husband. I have a high school diploma and am presently attending a local college, trying to obtain the additional education I need. My husband is a college graduate and a professional in his field. We are both attractive and, for the most part, respected and well liked. We have four children and live in a middle-class home with all the comforts we could possibly want.

"I have everything, except life without fear.

"For most of my married life I have been periodically beaten by my husband. What do I mean by 'beaten'? I mean that I have been hit violently and repeatedly; I have suffered painful bruises, bleeding wounds, and unconsciousness.

"When I say my husband threatens me with abuse I do not mean he warns me that he may lose control. I mean that he shakes a fist against my face, makes punching-bag jabs at my shoulder, or makes similar gestures which may quickly turn into a full-fledged beating.

"I have had glasses thrown at me. I have been kicked in the abdomen when I was pregnant. I have been kicked off the bed and hit while lying on the floor, again, while I was pregnant. I have been whipped, kicked and thrown, picked up again and thrown down again. I have been punched and kicked in the head, chest, face, and abdomen more times than I can count.

"I have been slapped for saying something about politics, for having a different view about religion, for swearing, for crying, for wanting to have intercourse.

"I have been threatened when I wouldn't do something he told me to do. I have been threatened when he's had a bad day and when he's had a good day.

"Now, the first response to this story, which I myself think of, will be, 'Why didn't you seek help?'

"I did. Early in our marriage I went to a clergyman who, after a few visits, told me that my husband meant no real harm. That he was just confused and felt insecure. I was encouraged to be more tolerant and understanding. Most important, I was told to forgive him the beatings just as Christ has forgiven me from the cross. I did that, too.

"Next, I turned to a doctor. I was given little pills to relax me and told to take things a little easier. I was just too nervous.

"I turned to a professional family guidance agency. I was told that my husband needed help and that I should find a way to control the incidents. I couldn't control the beatings. That was the whole point of my seeking help. At the agency I found I had to defend myself against the suspicion that I wanted to be hit, that I invited the beatings.

"I did go to two more doctors. One asked me what I had done to provoke my husband. The other asked if we had made up yet.

"I called the police one time. They did not respond to the call. Several hours later they called to ask if things had 'settled down.'

"I have nowhere to go if it happens again. No one wants to take in a woman with four children. Even if there were someone kind enough to care, no one wants to become involved in what is commonly referred to as a 'domestic situation.'

"No one has to 'provoke' a wife-beater. He will strike out when he's ready and for whatever reason he has at the moment. I may be his excuse—but I have never been the reason. I know that I do not want to be hit. I know, too, that I will be beaten again unless I can find a way out for myself and my children. I am terrified for them also.

"As a married woman I have no recourse but to remain in the situation that is causing me to be painfully abused. I have suffered physical and emotional battering and spiritual rape because the social structure of the world says I cannot do anything about a man who wants to beat me. But staying with my husband means that my children must be subjected to the emotional battering caused by seeing their mother's beaten face or hearing her screams in the middle of the night.

"I know that I have to get out. But when you have nowhere to go, you know that you must go on your own and expect no support. I have to be ready for that. I have to be ready to support myself and the children completely and still provide a decent environment for them. I pray that I can do that before I am murdered in my own home."

Unfortunately, Christine's experience is not atypical. She represents one of at least six million spouses or children who are violently attacked and battered each year by their husbands or other members of their families. With the possible exception of the military, more violence is committed within the family than in any other type of human group.

It Can Go the Other Way, Too

Of course some wives violently batter their husbands (as well as their kids). This can sometimes be triggered by stress or provocation with or without the influence of hypoglycemia, premenstrual syndrome, hormonally based mood cycles, or behavior patterns learned in childhood. Spouse abuse is not all one-way. However, often when the husband is attacked, it is after he has provoked his wife to the breaking point, and this represents a form of self-defense on her part. And the injuries and consequences of this female-to-male assault tend to be less serious than the reverse.

When we talk about battered wives, we are not talking about a shoving match or the isolated slap or punch but rather brutal beatings that occur frequently with serious physical damage and trauma inflicted upon the partner.

Why Do They Do It?

Why do men do this? And why do their wives remain in such painful, terrible marriages? What can the wife do? Can these men change? Will they accept help?

While it's impossible to obtain completely accurate statistics about how frequent the problem of violent physical spouse abuse is, we do know that 40 percent of all homicides in the United States involve spouses killing spouses. If we take a close look at the men who batter their wives, we find that they are not usually psychotic or psychopathic. They usually are ordinary men from all walks of life. What most of these men have in common is a low level of self-esteem, or insecurity, or a learned response, perhaps from childhood, of reacting violently when stressed. They often possess a very traditional concept of masculine and feminine behavior; they are often unusually jealous and possessive of their wives. When their masculine role is threatened they use their fists to assert and obtain power. They have to be in control.

Psychologist Donna Moore, author of *Battered Women*, has pointed out: "If the man comes from a home in which either his mother has been battered or he has been abused as a child, his earlier training and experience has taught him that physical violence is an acceptable response to anger. In other words, when children observe their mother being battered, they grow up assuming that this is the way men and women resolve their differences. Also, men who have been beaten as children have learned that the one who loves them has the right and often the responsibility to beat them (e.g., 'I wouldn't do this if I didn't love you.') These families are often the basic training grounds for teaching the acceptability of violence."

There is also evidence suggesting that the use of alcohol can give the batterer an excuse for the beating: "I was drunk when I did it." Thus alcohol excuses as well as helps precipitate an otherwise unacceptable behavior. Addiction to drugs such as cocaine, amphetamines, and PCP as well as some psychotic illnesses can also trigger violent behavior.

One curious thing about husbands who batter their wives is that they usually refuse to recognize that they have a problem and reject seeking outside help to control it. Why should they? If they are in the driver's seat, why get out? So they tend to refuse to accept responsibility for their violence. They may either minimize ("I really wasn't violent, all I did was slap her"), plead that it wasn't intentional ("I didn't mean to hurt her—I just wanted her to understand"), plead intoxication ("I was drunk—I don't remember a thing"), blame the wife ("It is really her fault—if she hadn't pushed me, it would have never happened"), or outright deny it ("I didn't do it—she's lying").

It is my observation that these men tend to be easily threatened, are very jealous, and feel a strong need to have power over their wives. Violence becomes a way of maintaining control. It is a learned behavior. It continues because it works and keeps working. The wife's cringing, crying, whimpering response powerfully reinforces it and greatly increases the probability it will happen again and again.

Why Women Stay

But why do wives put up with it? In fact they often hide it, going to considerable lengths to protect their husbands from outside retribution. This question is especially important because if women stay in such a relationship, repeatedly playing the role of victim, they greatly increase the risk that their sons will carry the same pattern into the next generation and in time abuse *their* wives. And it also increases the risk that their daughters will unconsciously seek out abusive husbands when they marry.

The three key reasons why most women remain in a home where they are continually battered is *fear, low self-esteem,* and *dependency.* The wife is financially, physically, and emotionally dependent on her husband. She usually is not employed and has small children. Her man is her only source of financial support. How can she survive if she leaves him? She also usually doesn't value herself. She has reduced self-confidence. Who else would have her? Since she does not like herself very much, she assumes most other people feel the same way about her. Her role as a woman even includes being in a bad marriage. To leave home would be to admit failure as a woman.

Fear also plays a role. The abusing husband often threatens extreme retribution upon his wife if she leaves him; he may threaten to take the children away from her. She becomes intimidated. She is also afraid to take action against him for fear of further beatings or even death. So she learns to play the role of victim. If she presses charges against her husband and he is arrested and locked up, it might result in his losing his job. How will bills be paid? And then when he gets out, what will he do to her then? Give him what he wants and maybe he will lay off. But this is an unrealistic fantasy. No matter how careful she is not to rile him, sooner or later he will again find some reason to vent his anger on her and beat her.

Another factor, noted by psychologist Lenore Walker, a researcher in the area of marital violence who has studied many battered women, is that sometimes after the beating the husband will be very contrite and apologetic, shedding tears and asking for forgiveness. He promises that this will never happen again. He may even lavish flowers, affection, and candy on her. She believes him. Her bruises have healed. But it is all just part of a cycle. The violence will shortly be repeated. Nothing has really changed at all.

What to Do?

The wife should understand that her husband's violence pattern will almost certainly be repeated. Promises mean very little. His intentions may be noble. But as with compulsive gambling, drinking, or drug use, when the tensions or jealousies build again, all his good intentions will be ignored. And the abuse will continue—there's never an end unless she acts.

Calling the police may temporarily (for a few hours or days) slow down the problem. But it does not stop or solve the husband's underlying violent tendencies. In fact it may only serve to provoke even more violent retributions when the officers are gone.

Specifically, what do you do? First you need to find a shelter where you and your children can go while you get legal counsel, psychological support, and safety for yourself and your kids. There are in almost every community special temporary havens or "safe homes" for battered women and their children to retreat to in an emergency. These locations are usually kept secret. So you need to do your homework first. Find out where to go. Call your YWCA, helpline, police department, or department of social services to find out where to go in an emergency. Then leave. Take the kids. He will not know where you are. By taking such action you stop playing the role of victim. You break the cycle. He no longer has total power over you.

The next most important thing that you have to do is find a support system. I have rarely seen the problem of family violence solved single-handedly by the one who is abused. You need someone who can give you more power as well as good advice. Someone whom you can totally trust, who can come to your aid, who will believe you. It could be your ecclesiastical leader. It might be a social service agency counselor. But it needs to be someone with whom you can have a continuing relationship and who will help you devise strategies for monitoring and coping with your husband's violence.

Then you need to make some key decisions. Do you want to get out of the marriage? Or do you want to see if counseling and therapy might save the relationship and help your husband eliminate his violent behavior?

He also has some decisions to make. Is he willing to receive therapy to eliminate his abusive behavior? Does he care that much about you, the family, and your relationship? In 80 percent of the cases I see, the husband *does not* want to lose the wife and kids and will enter counseling. But he will only do what he absolutely has to. No more. He will not voluntarily relinquish the power. He will not give one farthing more than is absolutely necessary. Thus it is imperative that there be leverage to motivate him to receive help. The two most powerful I know are the threat of losing his wife permanently via divorce (especially if you are already separated) and going to jail.

You Will Both Need Help

You may need a therapist who is behaviorally oriented, someone who will not be intimidated, who can practice tough love with both of you. You may need to be separated in the early part of the therapy. He'll need to earn his way back by consistently demonstrating responsible behavior. Strict consequences need to be set up if further violence were to occur—even if very minor. The experience of some suggests that anger control classes or therapy is most helpful when used along with regular marriage counseling in bringing about change and assisting the husband to face his violence tendencies. You may have to live apart during part of this healing period.

The abusive husband will quit being violent *only* if he absolutely has to. He can be in control if he wishes. He doesn't beat his boss up. Why? Because he would lose his job and be charged with criminal assault. In other words, the consequences would be too severe. Remember, a man beats up his wife because he can. Your husband needs to be fully aware that if he gets physical again, you do have some options. And there will be some uncomfortable consequences. You are not helpless. You do have a support system. And you do have a place to go.

If he chooses to enter therapy with you, there are a number of things that he can learn to do. He can be taught how to raise his anger threshold by progressive relaxation training; by using coping imagery, becoming desensitized to those cues which formerly triggered anger responses, role playing, and rehearsing appropriate responses to anger-provoking situations; and by assertiveness training where he is taught alternate (healthy) responses to frustrating situations, including dealing with put-downs, disagreements, and blunt criticism. He can learn to say no in a calm, persistent manner. He can also learn to express feelings without having to be violent at the same time. Cognitive restructuring is another helpful approach. This is a method of teaching the husband to see and interpret home situations in a new, less volatile way: "It's not worth it to get so angry" or "Getting upset won't help."

However, it may be that after many years of abuse you will have no interest in pursuing therapy with him or waiting for him. That is up to you. If he has been also seriously using alcohol or drugs, the chances of his changing permanently are greatly reduced. Your risks in returning to the relationship are much greater. I personally would not recommend going back to the relationship unless he became alcohol- or drug-free, no matter what. His willingness to give these up would be a good test of his commitment to change and would demonstrate how much he really loves you.

You may wish to place a restraining order on him so that he cannot visit the premises and disturb you. Most communities have special counseling groups for abused women which support you in dealing with your partner and in knowing what your legal rights are and where to get whatever special assistance you might need.

If you stay in a situation where abuse continues, the people who are hurt the most are your children. And the full damage may not show up until they marry and have children of their own. These kinds of problems get passed on from generation to generation by parent modeling and imitative learning. If you summon up all of your courage and strength, you can get out of it. You need not live in hell. If you don't have the strength to cope with your abusive husband, get into a women's therapy support group. Call the YWCA or social service agency to find where you can join such a group.

Good Prognosis

In counseling with men who are abusive, *where most of their other personal qualities are positive*, I have found a high rate of successful outcomes. Most don't want divorce. Most do love and need their wives. And a very high percentage of them are willing to enter some sort of treatment program with their wives—if they know they'll lose them if they don't.

In a way, I see these men as victims too—victims of inappropriate social learning as they grew up. So the challenge faced by both the husband and wife is to stop the sickness in this generation so that it doesn't get passed on to the children and grandchildren. Both need to know that the possibility of healing and cure really exists.

You can change. I see it happen all the time.

CHAPTER 15

Cheating and Infidelity:
When Trust Is Broken

When Sharon heard that her husband, Dick, was involved with Jennifer, she felt as if someone had slammed her in the solar plexus. It just could not be! Jennifer was one of her three best friends. They had known each other since junior high school. And she had done everything she knew to be a good wife to Dick and a good mother to their three children. Besides, her husband was on the board of elders in their church. He would never do anything like that! Or would he?

She felt empty, numb, abandoned. She felt angry, disillusioned, alone, and humiliated.

She suddenly realized that she was expendable. Not needed. Not loved anymore. The tears would come later, but now she was just shocked from an awful feeling of being rejected.

Why try to be a decent person? All it gets you is a kick in the teeth by someone you trusted, someone you thought you really knew.

Betrayal by someone you love is the bitterest and most galling of all human experiences. How could you ever trust anyone again?

To Sharon, even God seemed in hiding at this moment. She

was so hurt and felt so despicable, ugly, unfeminine, and un-wanted. Giant waves of insecurity and self-doubt washed over her. For a moment she contemplated a torrid affair with a bearded hip-pie to get back at him—she'd throw herself away! She would leave him with the kids! It would serve him right! But she immediately rejected it. That wasn't her. She could never do it.

What might cause a partner of fourteen years who once took solemn vows to honor, love, and forever remain true, to violate those sacred covenants?

As I have interviewed individuals who have been untrue to their partners (and current research suggests that about half of all married persons have cheated), I get a sense that when women do it, it arises out of acute dissatisfaction with the marriage or an unmet need for attention and affection. Whereas many men have affairs more often for lustful adventure, variety, or a boost to the ego. Furthermore, the unfaithful of either gender may be sex ad-dicts.

The Media Does Not Help

Best-selling novels, soap operas, movies, and much popular music deliver a powerful message that the only sex really worth having is either with someone else's spouse or in some way illicit or illegal.

Some popular sex manuals (as well as avidly read columns in men's magazines) are authored by prostitutes ("happy hookers"), brothel keepers, and occasionally even by a Ph.D. whose focus is to desensitize and give permission to the reader to perform any imaginable sex act. The theme is that anything goes, and—if you would believe them—with no apparent consequences.

While some of these manuals border on pornography, others present excellent scientific and useful knowledge about couple re-lationships and human sexuality. But some are value-free and es-pouse, essentially, total sexual license. Unfortunately, very little at-tention is paid to possible painful consequences of the behavior they endorse. These, of course, are the kinds of messages which all of us, including the husband of the aforementioned Sharon, are bombarded with daily.

The intent of some of this literature is in some ways very positive. At any given time something like 50 percent of all Americans suffer from some sort of sexual dysfunction, according to such experts as Masters and Johnson. These "total permission" books are written to reduce inappropriate guilt and to free many of their readers from the stultifying effects of negative conditioning about sex. But the pendulum has swung too far in the other direction. Usually these manuals mention nothing about medical and emotional complications that can include contagious venereal diseases, some not curable. They also have little to say about the painful consequences of breaking a trust (where partners are sexually cheating on each other), with its accompanying deception. In other words, the philosophy of some of this literature is "grab it while you can," a strictly short-term hedonistic viewpoint not unlike that of the drug abuser. Longer-term consequences are ignored. But the long term is always there, for all of us.

The Roots of Infidelity

In my decades of couple counseling I have found several primary excuses why people become unfaithful. Of course in any single instance there will be many contributors. But it might be helpful to identify and analyze some of these.

1. *The starved, unfed relationship.* Lack of sufficient communication, affection, or sex in marriage can leave a partner with many unfilled needs. They are starving. They often feel frustrated, rejected and empty. Communications may be impaired, if not by chronic fighting then by distance, coolness, and emotional isolation. There is no rapport. The whole marriage relationship is deteriorating. In this dangerous vacuum a friendship develops with someone with whom one regularly associates. Guess what? She has a similar problem. She feels unloved too. And this other person may gradually replace the spouse as the person to lean on and derive comfort from.

It is usually a gradual thing. Step by step it escalates. Initially, the person will deny to himself that he is involved or that he is having anything like an "affair." It is too decent. Aboveboard. But the mutual stroking continues. They feel valued, cared for. This is a very strong drug and a powerful affirmation experience. Then biology takes over. A quick embrace, hand holding, a kiss. Like the bee to the pollen, they go back for more. They're hooked—and the rest becomes history.

From a therapist's point of view, I place 75 percent of the responsibility for this problem on the shoulders of the needy partner, not vice versa. If you feel neglected or unfulfilled in any situation, you are more aware of this than anybody else is. It is up to you to take whatever steps are necessary to rectify it. It's really your problem.

2. *The momentary lapse.* Sometimes infidelity results from an accidental momentary encounter that happens at a vulnerable moment, perhaps after one has been traveling alone. While a serious breach of marital vows, it is transient and carries no powerful emotional bonding to the other person. Divorce and remarriage are not at issue for the errant partner. However, if the individual contracts VD, this can greatly complicate matters at home.

3. *The sexual addiction.* This represents a predictable compulsive pattern of promiscuity. This is an illness—a powerful addiction. In this situation the individual engages in a repeated series of one-night stands or brief affairs with many partners. Sex is a drug to him. He is heavily addicted; promises, good intentions, swearing on the Bible never to do it again mean nothing. It can happen to ministers, doctors, attorneys, college professors, plumbers, or sixteen-year-old boys. Their intentions may be the best, but they are out of control. Self-control and self-discipline don't work here. They truly lose their free agency. They cannot cure themselves. They have to have help.

For many years I have treated sexual addicts. It has been my experience that two things have to occur for them to get control of their lives again. They have to work with a therapist who has special training in treating this kind of illness. And they have to be in a twelve-step group similar to AA, or Alcoholics Anonymous. The group I use most often is SA, or Sexaholics Anonymous. It is anonymous. There are no costs or fees. These groups meet weekly in nearly every moderately sized or larger town in America. I have seen many marriages rehabilitated where there has been a long history of infidelity, with the erring partner becoming healed. The spouse needs help too, for she has been repeatedly traumatized and thus has enormous trust problems. But this can—if they both wish—all be worked through.

4. *Revenge.* Here the act of infidelity is a way of punishing one's partner, who may once have been unfaithful herself. It is a way of expressing anger and getting even, of trying to hurt one's partner for her past bad behavior. The feeling is, "If you did it, I can do it—I'll show you!" Retribution, not attraction, fuels this kind of infidelity. But in my experience, it usually turns out to be a joyless victory, with much guilt and a host of messy complications.

5. *Part of a liberated lifestyle.* Some people choose to have frequent affairs and highly variegated sex as part of a deliberately chosen value system. For them it is a matter of personal politics and values, a decision to live a life of open sexual experimentation free of commitments or exclusivity. Ordinarily, one has fair warning in getting involved with these types. So repeated infidelity should come as no surprise.

6. *Peer influence.* Some individuals who are fairly honorable, religious, or conservative can be influenced by close associates who encourage extramarital scoring: "Everybody's doing it. . . . Why not you?" "What the little woman doesn't know . . ." It may occur with a group of friends at a convention who all go to a porno or massage parlor. Or it could even be a group of suburban housewives sharing firsthand

the ups and downs of their current affairs. The constant association with others who engage in adulterous liaisons weakens one's normal restraints. With time a desensitization sets in which allows a rationalization to engage in activities previously regarded as unacceptable to one's standards.

7. *The emotionally unstable.* These include people who are schizoid, hypomanic, or, in more popular parlance, "flaky." They tend to have poor judgment and weak egos and are highly impulsive and easily seducible. They drift into illicit and illogical sexual liaisons with considerable frequency, primarily as a symptom of their emotional problems. Some of these people are pick-ups who nightly drift through the local bars seeking some kind of connection with other people. Because they do not discriminate, a high proportion have a history of venereal infection. They have very little to offer and are very high risks as marital partners. You can't depend upon them.

8. *The sociopath.* This is a person without significant conscience or ethical standards. Their life pattern involves cutting corners and cheating in everything they do. They are chronic and convincing liars. They can shed tears on cue if necessary to get their way. Frequently, they are very charming, bright, persuasive, and seductively friendly. They use these skills to con and manipulate people. They can be very convincing actors, appearing extremely sincere, but at heart they are loyal to no one but themselves, possess no integrity (though they'll claim otherwise), and do not know how to love. They care absolutely nothing about the pain or injury they cause others. They take what they want without regard for the grief they bring into the lives of those who trust and love them. A significant proportion of them abuse drugs and or alcohol. Sexually, they are takers and users. They say the right words but only as a technique for controlling others. They promise a lot but rarely deliver. *And they don't change!* The best way to understand them is to look at their past behavior, never at what

they say. Their past behavior is what will most accurately predict their future conduct.

9. *Good-neighbor Sam or Sally.* These are good people doing "good deeds" who sometimes get accidentally caught up in emotional involvements they cannot handle. It could be the minister counseling the lonely divorcée, or the boss trying to do some amateur marriage counseling with a troubled young employee. It always starts in a situation where someone who has a need develops a dependency on someone else. This may involve long private counseling sessions, which eventually lead to mutual admiration and later to hand holding, hugging, and eventually to bed—sometimes to their mutual surprise and chagrin. Freud called it transference and countertransference. It can happen to the nicest people we know. It is merely the natural man taking over when two healthy adults spend a lot of private time together, no matter how altruistic and noble their motives.

So What Do You Do About It?

If you or your spouse gets involved in such an illicit romance, what should you do? See your attorney and kick the bum out as soon as possible? Take the kids away so your spouse will not influence them with their sinful example? Hang around and see what's going to happen? Pretend not to know—just hope it will eventually blow away? Or see an ecclesiastical leader or a counselor and find out how to make things right and to strengthen and renew the marriage?

I've seen all of these responses many times. To give you good advice we need to back off and look at some general issues first.

First, *every* wife, even in the most superior marriages, has grounds for divorce. But so do all of their husbands. Every couple has some major areas of incompatibility and pain in their relationship. This is the nature of marriage. Meshing together two unique personalities into a compatible unit takes a great deal of commitment, years, effort, will, flexibility, and capacity to forgive. This never changes.

To live alone, however, can be even worse. It leaves one incomplete, unfulfilled, and unnurtured. Receiving and giving love in a balanced monogamous relationship is not easy—but it is worth it! No abundance of hit-and-run sexual partners can ever replace a rich long-term loving relationship built on trust, caring, affection, and good communication. Most "sexual freedom" advocates that I know eventually trade their lifestyles for a single committed relationship. They do it for pragmatic reasons—it simply works better. They find that sex with numerous partners is less satisfying than sex with one partner strengthened with trust and love. The price you pay for that is fidelity. Then you get loved in return. This is confirmed in *Masters and Johnson on Sex and Human Loving* where their research shows greater pleasure from marital than extramarital sex.

Marriage counselor Carlfred Broderick, a sociology professor at the University of Southern California, has commented in his book *Couples:* "The really rewarding experiences of life are to be found in trusting and enduring relationships. Certainty of another's commitment. These are profoundly satisfying things. Although I have seen the devastation that infidelity can bring, I have never come across anyone who has been destroyed by fidelity. I find it to be a cornerstone of successful marriage. I am impressed with the genuineness of the pain involved in marital boredom. But I am more impressed with the pain, the mistrust, the hurt, the shame, the guilt, and the feeling of being torn apart which are nearly always associated with the discovery of infidelity. There is no more distressing and divisive event in the relationship of a man and a woman than the disclosure that one partner has betrayed the trust of the other."

Getting into an illicit relationship is a little like getting hooked on a hard drug. It initially may feel great, but the price you pay is awful. In the midst of the affair the individual loses a certain amount of freedom of choice. The lovers are not entirely rational. Typically, they have an intense need for their paramour, but at the same time they are extremely anxious, guilty, and torn over losing their family. They flip-flop back and forth in a classic kind of ambivalence. They can't give up either; winning is losing; losing is losing; they go through hell.

Several years ago in my community, three physicians took their own lives when they saw no way out of this dilemma. The pain became more than they could endure. They discovered that if they were to eventually divorce and marry or live with the other women, they would quickly find that they had merely traded one set of problems for another. If they returned to their wives and families, it was like coming home after a tornado had struck. There was a tremendous mess to clean up and endless repair work to do. This reparation and restoration is not easy, but it is much preferred to the consequences of either letting the wounds of infidelity fester or taking one's own life. The healing and renewal of impaired relationships requires much patience and effort, and often skilled outside assistance.

The Consequences of Unfaithfulness

Everything in life costs. In my experience the cost of an affair is never worth it. Like cocaine or usurious interest, it exacts its pound of flesh to the *n*th degree. In a *Psychology Today* survey of twenty-five thousand of its readers, 45 percent admitted to cheating on their partners, but 98 percent saw monogamy and sexual exclusiveness as important to a committed relationship. No one enjoys living with an unfaithful mate, including those who are themselves unfaithful.

One thing that the "let's have great sex" books rarely ever mention is venereal disease. But it's out there and taking a toll with a vengeance. Some sexually transmitted diseases are incurable as well as very nasty. And I see too many instances where committed wives are being infected by promiscuous husbands (or vice versa). The complications this introduces into the trust bond are not pleasant to deal with. With AIDS now moving into the heterosexual population, the consequences of multiple infidelities for some people, as well as for their unborn children, may be lethal, a kind of Russian roulette.

The Predictable Cycle

I find that illicit affairs go through a predictable cycle. They are like illnesses. They have a course they follow. And they always come to an end—sooner, if they are discovered. Do you know of anybody whose affair did not eventually end? In most cases the individual does not marry the person he's involved with, even when he divorces his "impossible" spouse.

An affair usually starts out with a friendship phase, then romance, followed by an intense erotic bonding where the relationship escalates to its peak in excitement, desire, and sexual gratification. But from there it takes an irregular downhill course. Sooner or later one of the parties feels smothered and overcontrolled. Someone pulls back a little. There is a jockeying for power. There may be some lovers' quarrels followed by passionate make-up scenes. But it is never quite like it was in the beginning of the relationship. The partners begin to notice each other's inadequacies. Eventually one partner decides to end the relationship, either to return to the original mate or just get some breathing room. Again there is a protracted struggle of partings and making up. Throughout all of this, friends, family, and spouses have little influence. They can threaten, persuade, or cajole, but it will make little or no difference with the couple.

Sometimes I find it is best to counsel the other spouse to move with patience. As with the physically ill, the morally or spiritually sick may need to get over his fever and become rational before he can be dealt with. The quick divorce is not always the wisest way to go, even when the straying spouse appears beyond retrieval.

Three Things to Do

1. When you discover that your mate is adulterous I find it important to get it out in the open as soon as possible, with full disclosure for all parties concerned, including the lover's spouse. This permits an honesty—even though painful—that helps bring the deceit to a halt. Continuing deception is destructive to all parties. Confronting the issue allows you to get feedback on your deficiencies in the marriage that may have contributed to your partner's vulnerability. Also a "discovered affair" is rarely as exciting as one that is secret and high risk. Additionally, many times one party in the affair wants—maybe because of guilt—to

be discovered so she can terminate it and go back to her spouse. She feels somewhat trapped and does not quite know how to get out gracefully. Or she may be just plain weak or a "pleaser."

2. Next, carefully evaluate whether you wish to salvage the relationship and attempt to renew your love for each other. If your partner is "healed" and returns to normal, will he or she still have something that you can live with and love? Are there still a lot of positive qualities in your relationship? Make no final decisions at this time. Keep all of your options open. Just because your mate has been stricken does not mean the relationship is absolutely dead yet.

3. After the smoke has cleared (usually a few months later) and you have a good sense of where your errant partner is, it may be time to make a decision. There are probably three choices: (1) give the situation more time—do nothing; (2) rehabilitate your marriage and get counseling; or (3) terminate the marriage.

You can then choose a strategy that will be most effective in accomplishing the ends you seek. If you do decide on divorce, you need to ask yourself how this can be managed with the least damage to the children and yourself. If you decide to attempt to put the marriage back together again, you may need professional assistance. Choose that help wisely. Your spouse may not be ready for it, but there is no reason why you cannot start alone. This can help you develop wiser strategies later when you both work together on your marriage in earnest.

What If You Are the Unfaithful One?

If you are trying to put your marriage back together by working through some of your own blocks and obstacles, an affair is the last thing you need. An outside relationship (known or hidden) always changes the original marital relationship. It destroys your motivation and commitment to make your present marriage work.

Why should you struggle with problems of children, finances, and in-laws when your primary interest is a romantic adventure? Mostly, you don't, or you can't.

But if you were to marry your new paramour, in a short while you would be back to the same old problems of kids, finances, power struggles, sex, and in-laws. Romance and courtship are not marriage. They are not even comparable. In most cases I counsel that the grass that looks greener across the way turns out to be crabgrass.

Irene represents a typical case history which I see in my practice. As she put it, "Actually I had a very good marriage. But one day at work in walks this salesman. He was cute. He really turned me on. He made me feel so great. Soon we were having lunch together several times a week. As we got to know each other better, we soon realized that we had a marvelous intellectual and emotional rapport. When he kissed me one night late as I was closing the office I foolishly let myself respond with great passion. I fell in love with him. Absolute madness! But it happened. I left my great husband, got divorced, and eventually married this guy. It lasted only nine months. It was crazy. I left a good marriage for this flake who didn't have half of my husband's virtues.

"The strange thing is that while I was in it, it was like temporary insanity. Nobody, and I mean nobody, could tell me any different. All I knew was that he made me feel great. For a while that is. Until we got married. Then the balloon popped. I have nothing now."

Fidelity Is a Decision to Love

When infidelity occurs, most offended spouses feel that a basic trust has been violated. Sexual accessibility implies emotional accessibility. Commitment is now no longer assumed. Trust is an extremely important core ingredient that provides security, happiness, and stability in a relationship. When that is dissolved it radically changes the nature of the relationship. It can make one or both partners sick. It often brings forth latent heretofore hidden pathology such as paranoia. Or it can cause a profound chronic depression in one of the partners who often blame themselves for what has happened. A commitment to fidelity is not a prison and does not diminish freedom but rather represents a freely chosen decision to nurture a relationship. It represents a decision to love.

In love you are never "there." It is always an ongoing process, living, breathing, growing, or diminishing. It has to be constantly fed, tended, and nourished. The marriage ceremony is not the solution to a problem such as loneliness, or a goal to be reached, but rather it marks the beginning of a grand journey together into uncharted territory.

Masters and Johnson, in their book *The Pleasure Bond,* reported that among some educated people who consider themselves sophisticated, such words as *loyalty, faithfulness, honor,* and *trust* are avoided because somehow they seem suitable only for sermons. Yet all human associations depend on these and other such values, and they cannot be ignored in a marriage.

The commitment of sexual fidelity and trust between a couple is not a loss of freedom but rather an affirmation of a profound sense of security in a love relationship. This works both ways. It serves to protect our sanity, our happiness, and our understanding of ourselves as worthy people capable of being loved and sacrificed for. To love greatly requires openness and spontaneity. This can occur only in a situation of trust. We close ourselves off when we fear hurt. We role-play. We lose our genuineness. We are no longer real. However, in a state of commitment and vulnerability, love is, almost as a miracle, unfathomably regenerated.

As author-essayist C. C. Barbeau puts it, "Because true joy in sexuality depends on my ability to give myself totally, unreservedly, to you, our commitment by its nature involves sexual exclusivity."

CHAPTER 16

The Partner Who Abuses
Alcohol or Drugs

Being married to an alcoholic or one who abuses drugs can be a very painful and trying experience. If children are exposed to a parent who is an addict, the problems may become severely compounded. When even one spouse has this problem it becomes a family illness, because it damages and affects the entire family, not just the person who is addicted. Alcoholism is a progressive deteriorative illness which if not treated can end in death. To a greater or lesser degree the same is true for many other drugs. But all are treatable, and the key is obtaining the cooperation of the individual as early in the illness as possible.

The unfortunate fact of life is that most substance abusers don't want to give up their habit. They deny they have it. Or they deny its effects and blame others for their problems. Their addiction, in an ironic sense, is their psychological "blessing" but also their physiological curse.

Alcohol is the most abused drug in our society. And that's for three reasons: it is socially acceptable in nearly all parts of society; it is available everywhere; and for some, but not all, people it is highly addictive.

The psychological dynamics behind all addictions are very similar whether they involve cocaine, morphine, marijuana, tobacco, prescribed valium, or alcohol. Users get a high, or release from tension—initially a "quick fix." Then later, as they become more and more dependent on their drug, they use it to keep from hurting so bad. To some extent the same thing is true for compulsive gambling and sexual addictions. They offer a high with vivid and exciting memories. The temptation becomes overwhelming to repeat them in a compulsive way. But with repeated use of any drug the high gets weaker and the aftereffects get worse. So the person needs and uses more of the drug (or another like it) to get relief. This becomes the vicious circle of addiction.

With the more expensive hard drugs, many people eventually resort to selling them to support their own habit.

The modern pattern, especially with young adults in the United States, including many college students, is polydrug abuse. It is very rare to see a thirty-year-old alcoholic who is not also abusing a variety of other drugs. For most of them it has become a search for the super high, buzz, or rush, or more potent stress relief. And whatever is available they'll try. Prior inhibitions and prohibitions about using dangerous substances have already been violated so frequently that it is very easy to rationalize trying something new no matter how risky.

Always, in the beginning, there is the feeling of invincibility that "I can handle it; it can't control me," or "It's okay since I know when I've had enough."

Unfortunately, with polydrug abuse, when one is simultaneously using two or more substances, they can have a synergizing effect that makes their combined usage highly toxic and sometimes lethal. This has sometimes been referred to as the "Hollywood–death syndrome" because so many entertainment personalities have lost their lives this way.

Some Answers to Questions

Below are answers to some commonly asked questions about drug abuse. Since alcohol is the most abused drug, more emphasis will be given to it.

How many people drink alcoholic beverages? And how many alcoholics are there? Seven out of ten adult Americans occasionally or regularly drink alcoholic beverages. One out of ten of these is an alcoholic, or about nine million people.

What, exactly, is an alcoholic? These are persons (a) who cannot control their drinking—they are physically addicted to it—and (b) whose alcohol use causes problems for themselves, their families, and their jobs.

What are some of the cost figures on alcoholism? Fourteen billion dollars are spent yearly in medical and social costs. Five billion of these are for alcohol-related auto accidents. Half of all traffic deaths are alcohol related. Half of all murders and a third of all suicides involve alcohol. Nineteen billion dollars is lost annually in reduced job productivity. Then there are other kinds of costs that cannot be measured in dollars, such as potential damage to the fetuses of pregnant women who abuse alcohol, or the increased risk of later alcohol abuse by children who have lived with an alcoholic parent.

What physical damage can alcohol do to the body? First, alcohol is a classic example of empty calories (two hundred to an ounce); it not only lacks vitamins, minerals, and proteins but actually interferes with the body's ability to utilize the vitamins and other nutriments in what is actually eaten. So alcohol abuse can and often does lead to malnutrition. Many alcoholics have secondary diseases because they are so run-down nutritionally. In time, alcohol abuse can cause brain damage with destruction of neural tissue and loss of memory. It decreases brain protein synthesis, interferes with RNA, damages brain-cell membranes, and contributes to magnesium loss and cerebellar degeneration.

The chronic brain syndrome of alcoholism, Korsakoff's psychosis, leading to irreversible dementia (loss of intellect), memory impairment, and confabulation (thinking things are real that aren't) is another risk. In the sensitive lining of the gastrointestinal system, especially in the stomach, alcohol can cause gastritis and ulcers, pancreatitis, cirrhosis of the liver, disturbance of electrolytes and body-fluid balance. It is also a contributor to cancer, especially of mouth, esophagus, and stomach.

"Yes, but I have friends who drink like fish and have been doing this for years, yet they appear totally unaffected by their drinking." Not so! As with many other kinds of substance abuse the deteriorative effects are subtle and slow, and the individual for a time can successfully conceal these. But the laws of nature are immutable. And the body knows what's been consumed no matter what the story reported to a husband, wife, friend, or doctor has been.

Also, we all know people whose heavy drinking has raised havoc with their careers or even contributed to their early death.

Is alcoholism a disease? While there is some debate on this, the best answer is probably yes. It is the number-three killer in the country (after heart disease and cancer) and the number-one health problem. Alcoholics do not get better unless the alcoholism—not some underlying cause—is treated directly.

What, exactly, is alcohol? It is a substance called ethanol in chemistry. The formula is C_2H_2OH and is the key ingredient (along with water) found in all intoxicating beverages from the most expensive scotch to the cheapest wine. It is a colorless, almost odorless, flammable, volatile liquid with a burning taste. It is a sedative, a hypnotic, a tranquilizer, a narcotic, sometimes a hallucinogen, or an anesthetic, and it is dangerously addictive to some but not all people. It has been called the world's greatest tranquilizer.

Alcohol has a double-acting effect. It first gives an apparent lift (mainly psychological) by depressing the inhibitory centers of the brain while providing quick caloric energy. This is followed by a sedative action. If enough is consumed, it can lead to drunkenness, unconsciousness, or even death.

How long does it take for alcoholism to develop? Typically, from seven to twenty-five years with the average around fifteen; however, with young people it can occur much more quickly.

How do I know whether my spouse ia an alcoholic or may be in danger of becoming one? They will have some of the following symptoms: (1) One or both parents were alcoholic—there is an inherited vulnerability to it, with males being especially high-risk. (2) They drink excessively as a matter of necessity, not choice. They may lie about how much they are actually drinking, and they cannot stop after just one or two drinks. (3) They have blackouts (amnesia) where they cannot remember what happened to them during periods when drunk. (4) They are sneaking drinks, gulping drinks, or drinking alone. (5) They deny that they have a drinking problem, in the face of much contrary evidence. They lie (understate) about how much they are consuming. (6) They begin to ignore family, financial, job, and other responsibilities. (7) They show a decreasing interest in nondrinking activities. (8) They lose time from work or school because of drinking. (9) They have one or more drunk-driving arrests in a year. (10) They need a drink "the morning after" and before going to bed to cure the shakes. (11) They make promises to quit drinking but break them. (12) Personality changes begin to occur: they become irritable, tense, forgetful, hard to get along with.

Why is it so hard for the alcoholic to kick the habit when the consequences are so negative for everybody? First, the individual has a chemical addiction: there are actual cellular body changes that have caused a significant chemical dependency on alcohol. Without alcohol they experience severe withdrawal symptoms. Second, for brief periods the alcoholic can cut down on or even briefly eliminate his intake, but when stress of any kind occurs, alcohol is again the solution. Alcohol and drugs work. There is no waiting. They knock out anxiety, tension, loneliness, and boredom. They offer an escape from problems and stress. And they do this instantly. Nothing works as well or as fast. But it has a price. After a while the abuser needs it to fall asleep, to face the new day, to deal with a spouse, to handle an important business deal, or to enjoy a social event. The third reason it is so hard to quit is the universal tendency for alcoholics to *deny* they have a problem. They refuse to accept responsibility for the fact that they have a serious addiction.

One of the most difficult things alcoholics have to deal with is the powerful memory they have of the relief and good feeling drinking gives. Learning good communication skills to work out difficult and challenging marital problems takes a lot of effort and work. Two whiskey sours is so much quicker. It does not solve the marital problem, but it makes the drinker feel so much better about it. And when someone is discouraged and hurting, that is what counts.

Is it possible to cure alcoholics? No. They can only be in remission. But if they do not drink they can live normal productive lives.

Can an alcoholic ever learn to drink moderately? Not really. At least not in most cases. Just as the compulsive gambler can never handle even a little gambling or the morphine addict even a little morphine, the alcoholic cannot be a moderate drinker. Total abstinence has been found to be the only workable solution to the problem of alcoholism.

What about other drugs? While we have focused on alcoholism, most alcoholics, especially if young, abuse other drugs, too. These include amphetamines, cocaine, heroin, PCP, LSD-like psychedelics, marijuana, glue or solvents, or a variety of prescribed medications such as valium, barbiturates, codeine, or morphine-type pain killers.

Of these, cocaine might be considered the drug of the nineties. It increases energy and self-confidence, making you feel like Superman (or woman). The bad news is that there is a very high addictive component to cocaine users; users can develop an intense craving for more. And it is very expensive. Cocaine, along with some amphetamines, is the drug most eagerly self-administered by experimental animals who will kill themselves with voluntary injections. I have had patients tell me that it was harder for them to get off of cocaine than heroin. And it later produces symptoms of irritability, anxiety, paranoia, insomnia, perceptual distortions, disturbed concentration, elevated blood pressure, accelerated heartbeat, delusions, and hallucinations. In some situations it can cause aggression and crime. When combined with other opiate-type drugs (as in a speedball) and taken intravenously it can in some cases cause death. The *Comprehensive Textbook of Psychiatry*, 4th edition, quite succinctly sums it up, "The financial, physical, and psychological costs of compulsive cocaine use can be devastating."

Can cocaine abuse be overcome? Yes—but it is not easy. Paul and Paula were a fast-track college-educated couple who started abusing cocaine. When the practice got out of control it devastated them financially and threatened their marriage. One day they both knew that they had to face their addiction. Too many bad things were happening. They knew that nothing but destruction lay ahead if they continued as they had been doing. It took them three years with many setbacks, but they finally became free of cocaine. It required them to move and to change jobs and friends. In overcoming it, they worked as a team—when one was down the other was there to pull them through the bad days and nights. But they did it!

I'm married to an alcoholic and drug user—what do I do? What you should do will depend on how serious their problem is. How out of control are they? To what extent is it disturbing the marriage or interfering with their ability to hold a job, pay their bills, and be generally responsible? And how rapidly are they deteriorating? And, if they recognize it as a problem, are they willing to get some help? Is it something they have to have no matter what? Is their use of it wrecking the budget? Is one partner being physically abused? Are they borrowing large sums of money with no possible way of paying it back? Is there risk, because of the people they are associating with, that they could escalate to rougher, more dangerous drugs?

When people start getting immersed in the drug culture it cuts them off from contact with "straight" friends. It changes their values and lifestyle as it becomes necessary for them to engage in illicit activities to get money to support their drug needs. A $150-a-day habit forces them to do illegal and immoral things. Do any of these apply to your spouse?

One of the major problems in dealing with drug and alcohol abusers is that they deny they have a problem nearly to the end. They may admit they drink or use drugs some—but no more than most other people. Not true. And if you are upset about what they are doing, they will tell you that it's *your problem,* not theirs, and if they are not upset about it, why should you be? It is usually impossible to reason with them about the issue. You'll never win an argument about it. Their minds are made up. They are not interested in what you have to say. They usually are going to do what they want to do regardless of the outcome. The issue is nonnegotiable.

What Side of the Line Are They On?

There exists an invisible line that separates mild drug or alcohol use and true abuse and addiction. If your spouse is on the safer side of this line, then you are dealing with risks only and with a possible mild challenge if you want to get them to quit altogether. This situation is usually negotiable. But if they have crossed over the line and are hooked, *you will not, by yourself, be able to save them.* Tears, threats, sex—nothing will work to get them to quit. The only thing that you might do, if you are extremely lucky, is to motivate them to go in for treatment.

Even when they choose to get treatment it usually takes two to five years to wean an alcoholic or a drug addict from their habit. And along the way there will probably be a few relapses. It is almost never a straight, easy path. In my experience it has been absolutely critical for the individual to have a support system (such as Alcoholics Anonymous) to nurture, care, and "tough love" them through the many months and years of needed therapy. On the other hand, spending $10,000 for several weeks in an aversion-therapy treatment center does not always seem to work very well. These treatments have high relapse rates, probably due to their lack of long-term, well-defined support groups and follow-through. But it could still be a place to begin the journey back if you have the funds or insurance to pay the bill.

Not a Cure, but a Solution

In treating drug addictions one is never cured. At best the illness can only be in remission. Sobriety is maintained a day at a time through abstinence. This is not to say that some addicts do not manage to stay free and healthy the remainder of their lives. This is certainly possible. But they can never say, "Now I'm out of danger," or "It's no longer a problem." They always have to be on their guard.

In my practice, I sometimes recommend first detoxification in an in-patient treatment center, followed by individual therapy plus group therapy (with AA or an equivalent organization). The particular treatment strategy will depend on the type of drug abused and how emotionally disturbed the individual is. Many drug abusers have serious emotional problems underlying their addiction which also need attention. The therapeutic strategies used will depend on the nature of these problems and the resources available to the addict and you—the spouse who is *not* the abuser will also need help, especially if he or she chooses to stay in the relationship.

Your Two Choices

If you have a spouse who is a serious abuser living with you, you have two choices. Stay with them trying to be as helpful as possible. Or separate, especially if they refuse to accept any responsibility for getting help, are abusive to other family members, or are irresponsible, spending the kids' lunch money on their habit and so on, or are generally impossible to live with.

Whether you choose to let them stay or leave, I have some suggestions about handling the situation and relating to them:

1. Don't ever drink or use drugs along with them.
2. Don't ever shield them from the consequences of their alcohol or drug use. Don't go on "rescue missions" to bail them out of jams or save them from crises. It will just prolong the day of their recovery. This will also weaken their desire to do something about their problem. They will not recover as long as other people remove the painful consequences of their drinking or drug use!
3. Don't take over their responsibilities. If they miss half a day's work, let *them* handle it—*never* do it yourself.
4. Join AL-ANON (or the drug equivalent), which is for friends and families of alcoholics. This is especially important for you to do if they refuse to get help. Look up the number in the phone book. It is a companion organization to Alcoholics

Anonymous. It is there to give you long-term support and understanding at a very difficult time in your life.

5. Learn the facts about alcoholism and other drugs you may have concerns about. There are a number of community agencies with many free booklets and other information. Devour them. Become the world's greatest expert. These will help you understand the problem better as you make good decisions for the future.

6. Accusations and empty threats directed toward your spouse never work. "Tough love" does. Be prepared to act. If your alcoholic spouse refuses to be treated, you may need to leave or ask them to leave. With "tough love" you are not mean—you actually help them. But you do set limits and negotiate consequences. And you don't waver on these at all.

7. Face the truth. Don't refuse to face up to the illness in your home. The truth is, if your spouse is abusing alcohol or drugs, it will be as damaging to the whole family as it is to your spouse. This is a family illness. Everybody is affected!

8. If your partner blames you for their problems, remember, this is typical and predictable. Don't be conned or intimidated by this argument. It's a manipulation technique designed to make you feel guilty and responsible for their problem—and take the heat off them.

9. You will probably need to get marriage counseling. A spouse who abuses drugs or alcohol *always* creates problems for the marriage.

10. If your spouse tells you that they would not have their problem if they just had the right job, or that if you were just more responsive sexually, or if you were less critical or more supportive, this, again, is manipulation. If they had all of these things, nothing would change. It is just part of the denial game. If you were so foolish as to buy into it, it would further delay their getting well.

Your Objective: Getting Them into Treatment

If your partner denies that he or she has a drug or drinking problem, say, "Let's make an agreement. If you can limit yourself to one drink a day (or the legal drug equivalent) you'll get no hassle from me. But if you *ever* go over that *even once*, you then go in for treatment, okay?" If they agree to that, you both win. Because if they are *not* true alcoholics, they *will* be able to easily abide by the agreement (and you may thus be able to get them to eventually abstain). If they are out of control, they won't be able to keep the agreement, and then, hopefully, they can be convinced to receive the needed treatment.

But you can't tolerate any excuses. Not a single one. If, for example, they break their promise and do abuse alcohol or drugs, then you have to insist on their getting into a treatment program. If they refuse, you may have to move out or have them move out. If you tolerate broken agreements, you both lose!

Also, be aware that when people give up an addiction, they need something positive to replace it with, to plug in the hole. It could be an exciting hobby, learning to fly a plane, joining a physical-fitness club, becoming active in religious functions, jogging, belonging to a square-dance group, finding more satisfying employment, or having a much more fulfilling marriage. But there clearly need to be substitute "fun activities" that make the person feel good, that fill their deepest needs, and that bring balance back into their life.

CHAPTER 17

Depression in the Relationship:
What to Do

If you have a chronically depressed spouse, you have a marriage
in trouble. So how do you assist them? How do you help pull them
out of the pit?

When I saw Madeleine, she was forty with three teenagers and a
schoolteacher husband. The past year had been spent in her bedroom with the blinds drawn, door locked, and blanket and pillow
pulled over her head. Weeks' worth of cereal dishes and empty milk
cartons were stacked up in the kitchen; the house was unvacuumed
and littered with debris. She was so depressed she could not even
cry. She had become totally immobilized and nonfunctional.

It is not easy to live with and love someone who is depressed.
They have nothing to give, and you carry the full load.

In understanding depression, it is important to realize that
there are different kinds. And the most helpful treatment depends
on which kind you or your spouse may have.

At least twice as many women have bouts of depression as
men. Only one in five depressed individuals will get any kind of
treatment, and only one in fifty will require hospitalization.
Among young people with depression 95 percent recover within a

month. Depression is considered by some to be the "common cold" of mental illness; we all on occasion are afflicted, but most of us get well before long.

Depressive symptoms show up in four areas of functioning:

1. *Feelings.* We feel dejected, helpless, mournful, empty, futile, apathetic, and filled with despair.

2. *Thoughts.* We may engage in pessimistic thinking, have a poor self-image, concentrate poorly, feel guilty, think about suicide, and have a negative view of ourselves, the outside world, and the future; we experience learned helplessness—"No matter what I do, it doesn't make any difference; I'm powerless." There is a loss of interest, reduced motivation, impaired thinking, indecision, and feelings of incompetence.

3. *Behavior.* We may be either sluggish or agitated, neglect our personal appearance, withdraw socially, talk less, refuse to solve problems—we may even attempt suicide. In extreme cases we may become nearly totally immobilized.

4. *Physiology.* We may experience a loss of appetite, diminished interest in sex, sleep disturbances, a lack of facial expression, a slowing down of all body movements, chronic fatigue and weakness, constipation, aches and pains.

Nobody who is depressed will have all of these symptoms at one time or in an equal degree. This will depend on the severity of the depression.

Here are some of the major types of depression that we or one of our family might experience in the course of our lifetimes:

1. *Normal depression.* This occurs as a reaction to some stressful or painful event, a loss or disappointment. A family member has died; we get fired from our job; our lover jilted us; some hit-and-run crunched our new car while we were shopping at the supermarket, and we have no insurance.

So we feel miserable because of what has just happened to us. But in a few days we will snap back. We will handle it. Life moves on, and we leave the depression behind. The depressed feelings we had were actually quite appropriate to the situation. In fact, if we *hadn't* felt a little bad, that itself would have been abnormal.

2. *A neurotic depression.* Sometimes bad things happen in our life, and we get depressed and don't bounce back. We stay depressed. And this goes on with minor variations for months, maybe years. But we are still able to hold our job, take the kids to Little League, fix dinner for guests—even though it's not easy. This is a kind of depression we learn to live with, albeit rather miserably. And because we cannot shake it, we feel very sorry for ourselves. Often the sympathy we get from others tends to reinforce the maintenance of this depression. There is a neurotic "holding on" quality to this. Most neurotic depressives love to play the role of victim and martyr because it "hurts so good." Many are "injustice collectors." They never really recover, because if they look hard enough they find an awful lot of things out there to feel bad about, and there are usually some kind of significant payoffs for them.

Its origins are nearly always in childhood growing-up experiences where there was a history of rejection, maybe even abandonment or long-term lack of being sufficiently nurtured or loved. Thus it is a kind of learned sadness. And thereafter we often feel unloved, not wanted, and not able to make intimate connections. In a sense it is a learned depression or sadness.

Mrs. Hodges, wife of a prominent surgeon, found that if she was feeling ill her husband would pay more attention and spend more time with her. So she never got around to feeling better. This depression was not a deliberate deception, but a primarily unconscious one.

A neurotic depression is a chronic emotional illness that rarely gets better spontaneously. And while there may be some good days, most are bad. Treating it will require a combination of psychotherapy and, in some instances, anti-depressant medication.

3. *A major unipolar depression.* This is a moderate to severe depression which in some cases can incapacitate us. More women than men have it. And in most cases it will eventually leave even if untreated. The evidence suggests both situational and genetic factors can contribute to its occurrence. Some of our relatives usually have it too. This depression sometimes occurs regardless of what is happening in our lives. We could have just won a million dollars in the state lottery and still feel terrible. It is, in part, apparently triggered by imbalances of neurotransmitter chemicals, such as norepinephrine and serotonin, in the brain. A combination of antidepressant medication and psychological therapy seems to be most helpful with this kind of depression.

4. *A bipolar manic-depressive illness.* This depression is typically characterized by high and low mood swings, which, if extreme enough, can incapacitate us and make it difficult to hold a job or manage family affairs. On the high end of the cycle are euphoria (feeling invincible and all-powerful but with very poor judgment) or even manic feelings and behavior. And on the other end are states of profound despair. Some people will emphasize the high end or low end for most of their symptoms, so the swings might be high to normal or low to normal and back again. The evidence suggests that this is also a biological problem with inherited genetic contributors, which best responds to lithium-carbonate medication. It is, to a considerable degree, impervious to what is happening in the environment. Because it is a chemical imbalance in the brain, talking therapy alone is not effective.

Most depressions are curable or will spontaneously disappear given a little time, though they may reoccur at a later time. Unfortunately, when medications are used, most take three to four weeks to relieve symptoms.

I have seen spouses who have become depressed because they felt unloved in their marriage. Or because of constant conflict or rejection by their partner. Or in some cases because communication was so poor. Or they received almost no positive reinforcement in their day-to-day relations with their spouse. This would probably be considered a normal depression, but unless the pattern of the marriage relationship changes it could go on indefinitely. The solution here is not so much drugs or individual psychotherapy but a change in attitude and behavior and an increase in maturity by both partners in the relationship.

The medications which have been found to help most with depression belong to several different chemical families: the SSRIs (Prozac, Zoloft, etc.), the tricyclics and tetracyclics (Elavil, Tofranil, etc.), the MOA inhibitors (Marplan, Parnate, etc.), and lithium carbonate, plus some newer unique medications just being approved for use in the United States.

With such medical treatment, there is a delay of several weeks before you will see any noticeable relief. The major exception to this is a nondrug treatment, electroshock therapy, which induces an instant effect but sometimes causes temporary memory loss (which may be one of the reasons it works). There are also new medications, like Effexor, which tend to act very quickly but about which we have less information as to their short- and long-term side effects.

None of these chemical therapies ever solve any of life's problems. But they can in their own way make living a little more comfortable and reduce the risk of suicide.

My preference is to first try short-term psychotherapy alone, also addressing the problems of living and reducing the stresses in our lives. For many depressives this will be sufficient. Recent National Institutes of Mental Health–funded research suggests that talking therapy is every bit as potent as any of the standard antidepressant medications in relieving depressive symptoms. However, a wise strategy might be, if necessary, to use a combination of medication plus psychotherapy. This seems to produce the quickest results for certain kinds of depressed patients. It is sometimes necessary to adjust the dosage of the medication or even try several different kinds in order to find exactly the right mix for a

particular patient. Where medication is required, a physician familiar with antidepressant medication and its side effects should be
retained to prescribe appropriate dosages.

In summary, if you are depressed, you need not be. There are
solutions for most people. They won't solve all your life's problems, but you can certainly be more comfortable and feel better.
It's your choice.

CHAPTER 18

Living with a Neurotic or Emotionally Unstable Spouse

While there are many kinds of neurotic people, anxiety, in one form or another, is at the core of all of their symptoms.

They will never be crazy. They can hold a job or raise children. But they all suffer! And if you have to live with them, they will see to it that you suffer right along with them.

Typical Kinds of Neurotic Behavior

Some common examples of neurotic behavior include the housewife cleaning and scrubbing till two in the morning for fear that some neighbor might suddenly knock on the door and find her home dirty and unacceptable. Or there is the bank teller who has counted that roll of pennies eleven times for fear that he might be off one in his count, which, to him, would be intolerable. What would his boss say if he found out he had made a mistake? Then there is the hypochondriac who is always telling you about his back or head pain or fatigue, or swollen glands, and knows that his days are numbered. Or the tense, fidgety, uptight boss, mother, or grandfather with the strained look who is always waiting for some sort of catastrophe. They are worry-warts. And nobody is going to change them, no matter how convincing the evidence.

Harold constantly feared imminent financial collapse despite a well-paying job and substantial savings. He was so penny-pinching that his wife and children wore only second-hand clothes purchased at thrift stores. Their furniture was worn. Harold's constant response to any request for money from his wife was (delivered with a worried expression), "We just can't afford it now. Our situation is very serious!"

Myrna kept imagining that her children might be injured or killed by all sorts of dangers. So she denied any request by them to visit friends, climb trees, or go to the park or to a summer camp. In time her anxious concern infected the children, and they became chronically fearful too.

Mary Ann would lock her children out of the house during all daylight hours. She feared that they would bring in dirt and clutter up her home. Then the neighbors might think she was a poor housekeeper. She shoved out food through a little "doggy hole" in the back door. Her house stayed immaculate as she waxed and scrubbed day and night.

An elderly widow was devastated when, at a certain point during church services, an obscene word would flood her mind. She felt extremely ashamed and mortified knowing that God would feel most displeased and angry at this mental blasphemy. No matter how hard she tried, she could not rid her mind of this obsessional thought. She always left the services in tears of remorse until she finally sought help.

Neuroses are all learned, though there is some evidence to suggest that some people inherit temperaments and nervous systems that are more vulnerable to this kind of learning. In other words, some people have more tender psyches. They damage easily. They are like my foreign car. Lean on it and you have a dent. This is why children in the same family handle trauma, stress, or sick and devastating environments differently. Some are more resilient; some more fragile. They are born that way. But the bottom line of neuroses is that these illnesses develop out of painful life experiences which leave an imprint on us. However, anything that is learned can be unlearned. And that is what a healing environment and psychotherapy are for.

In the case of phobias, one is fearful of a thing, place, or situation. It might be elevators, high places, crowds, spiders, asking someone for a job, speaking in public, or certain aspects of sex. Or one may have low self-esteem. They may have a low-grade neurotic depression—the world is always "falling in," the worst is about to happen! Or they might have obsessive, uncontrollable thoughts such as a fear of injuring or killing someone they love, or unacceptable sexual thoughts. But whatever it is, one thing is certain: they experience a lot of distress for unrealistic reasons. Or if they do have legitimate reasons to worry about something, their anxiety is exaggerated out of proportion to the seriousness of the situation. And even if they recognize that it doesn't make sense to feel the way they do, they cannot help it. You cannot reason them out of it.

Neuroses also can be experienced as a generalized "free floating" kind of anxiety that pervades their whole being. They are anxious, although they are not sure why. They may find it difficult to make decisions about even such things as which coat to wear. They fear they will make a mistake. They ask others for advice and are then afraid to accept it.

Other kinds of neurotic disorders include converting psychological stress into physical symptoms such as ulcers, hives, headaches, paralysis, and even, in some traumatic cases, partial blindness or loss of memory. One might even have a psychogenic pain problem where severe pain in any part of the body may have an entirely psychological origin. A persistent, nagging depression may have a neurotic or psychogenic origin.

How to Live with a Neurotic Spouse

Neuroses can be minor, moderate, or severe. And their intensity can vary from time to time depending on the stresses in the environment at a given moment. A disturbed marital relationship will probably add to someone's neurotic problems. It will make the affected person even more insecure and off balance and less able to cope with their neurosis.

If you have a neurotic spouse, it is important to realize that, for the most part, their illness is not really their fault. Life is kind of a gauntlet: some of us get through without much trauma or damage, others get clobbered—and when we do, we pay a price. We get scarred. We may become neurotic or in some other way emotionally damaged. We are then forced to deal with that neurosis or problem the best way we can.

So, my bias is that if we are married to a neurotic, we need to have some compassion and understanding because it could have been any of us. This does not mean that we baby them or reinforce all of their "silly neurotic complaints." But we can be responsible and reasonable in helping them deal with their pain. There is a very delicate balance between having a genuine concern and sympathy for our spouse's neurotic problems and foolishly rewarding them for being ill by doing *everything* for them or showing such excess pity that we unwittingly encourage their behavior because they receive so much attention. This may sound like "tough love"—and that's exactly what it is.

Next we might mention that there are many antianxiety medications available through a doctor's prescription. But there is good news and bad news about them. While they can make one feel more comfortable, most have somewhat noxious side effects and can be chemically or psychologically habit forming. Long-term dependence on them never solves out-there-in-life problems. So they must be used with caution. Abuse or overdependence on these medications can create greater problems than the original neurosis.

Sometimes antidepressant medications have also been found useful in treating neuroses—especially where depression is a part of the problem. But the same cautions regarding their use apply here as with the antianxiety medications.

There are four major approaches in psychotherapy that I find most helpful in treating neurotic people. These can be used either individually or in combination:

1. *Behavior Therapy.* This approach sees neuroses as learned behavior. It focuses on treating neurotic symptoms directly, using the technology of experimental learning theory. Thus, a phobia might be treated via a desensitization technique.

2. *Cognitive Therapy.* This approach focuses on correcting irrational thinking and distorted beliefs and perceptions as a way of healing certain kinds of neurotic disorders. Some kinds of depression are caused by false ways of perceiving one's life experiences. Change these perceptions, and the depression may be dramatically diminished.

3. *Family Systems Therapy.* This approach views the family and any sick members in it as an interrelated system. It requires changing the whole family system in order to heal its individual members. A juvenile drug addict may be hospitalized, treated, and temporarily give up drug use, but if he goes back to the same sick family system, the cure may not last.

4. *Relaxation and Stress Management Therapy.* Stress is seen here as a major contributor to many illnesses. Successfully managing and controlling stress is vital to symptom relief across a broad range of psychological and physical illnesses. In the last ten years a remarkable array of progressive relaxation and stress-reduction techniques have been developed and successfully used with patients. Some have made use of biofeedback, imagery training, life-change management, anger control, assertiveness training, exercise, and even proper nutrition and weight control.

A fifth kind of therapy approach is to have the neurotic person join a *no-fee co-dependency twelve-step support group.*

Such approaches as psychoanalysis or even some of the long-term insight therapies are currently less in vogue, mainly because they are expensive, time-consuming, encourage dependence, and do not work that well.

Some neuroses are not easy to treat. In fact, neurotic character and lifestyle for the most part are extremely difficult to cure through self-discipline alone, becoming informed through a stack of self-help books, or just gaining insight into your problems, although all of these approaches can help.

You may get some improvement with therapy. But many patients are reluctant to give up their symptoms, as they love to talk endlessly about them. They often get many rewards from having them (often not readily apparent to the outside observer) and hence hang on to them despite everything done for them.

The biggest therapeutic hurdle is to motivate the neurotic patient to take some responsibility for getting well. This is why a responsible balance between charitable concern and "tough love"—a kind of middle-of-the-road approach that does not overindulge them with their many complaints—is the best way to go on living with them.

A deeply neurotic patient requires the skills of an exceptionally understanding spouse or an able therapist to help him or her overcome the symptoms and move forward to a more productive life. But it is possible. It will not happen overnight, and it will require a great deal of patience and understanding from the partner.

CHAPTER 19

Psychological Allergies in Marriage: The Poison Ivy Spouse

Jack, a computer programmer, had been married for twelve years. He had three lovely children and Cindy, a great wife and mother. All except for the fact that Cindy in recent months had become allergic to him—not physically, but psychologically. He was like poison ivy to her. She couldn't stand him. She could not tolerate the sound of his voice nor would she allow him to touch her.

She felt somewhat guilty about this because they were still living together and he was still her husband. He was a good father and provider. He never abused her. She was also very much aware that he had a very strong sexual drive. If she didn't satisfy this need, he might start looking elsewhere. Was that what she wanted? But she still felt what she felt! When he touched her she got sick to her stomach. And she didn't fully understand the reasons.

She found herself overreacting to everything he said or did. An innocent request became an outrageous demand; a mild suggestion seemed like the harshest kind of criticism. A simple correction unleashed in her a raging torrent of abuse toward the man who a few years ago she had vowed to eternally love and cherish. She got an almost malicious pleasure out of fighting with him. She didn't understand why she felt this way and why she did these things to her husband. But she still continued to do them.

A psychological allergy can be slight, moderate, or severe. It can go either or both ways in a relationship. It can also develop with a person at work or a neighbor down the street. It can happen between parent and child in either direction. Its essential core, in marriage, is a supersensitivity to one's partner. It's emotional, initially beyond rational control. All you know is that you feel this way—it's a "falling into hate," just the opposite of falling in love. Your partner becomes your adversary. Mild suggestions are interpreted as major attacks which are to be resisted or confronted vehemently. It is like having a pebble in your shoe which after a while feels like a giant jagged rock—which is your mate.

I have seen cases where this psychological allergy actually also became a physical allergy. If one partner even touched the other, this person broke out into hives or a rash. This ruined sex and required sleeping in separate beds.

When psychological allergies occur, the other partner frequently becomes bewildered by their spouse's extreme rejection of them for no apparent reasons. Nothing makes sense. A rational discussion of the issue gets them absolutely nowhere. It has become a no-win situation: everything they do is wrong. Just being there is wrong. They try to cope by following different kinds of strategies, without avail. Saying nothing appears to provoke further combat: "Open your mouth, dummy—you're just like your mother, a snivelling coward, afraid to discuss the situation. I hate you when you just stand there and say nothing. Speak! Speak!"

But what to say? The rejected partner feels like he or she is crawling through a loaded minefield where the slightest misstep will bring all hell raining down. This, of course, is no fantasy but exactly what happens.

The Origins of Psychological Allergies

Where do these negative feelings come from? In my studies of many couples afflicted with this "disease," I often find that the roots of a psychological allergy go back to childhood conflicts, rejection or abuse by one or both parents or parent-surrogates, or

even the bad things that happened in a prior marriage. These feelings can be accidentally reactivated by one's present mate during
periods of stress. It's like accidentally ripping the scab off of an old
wound. Repressed hates, fears, and angers are traumatically
reawakened. These often stem from unresolved conflicts, usually
with parents or a person of the opposite sex. I find them to be
mostly unconscious. They reside deep within the psyche, un-
acknowledged but smoldering for many years, only to one day suddenly explode into the present relationship.

If the rejected partner reacts in a similar manner, tit-for-tat and
blow-for-blow, this confirms to the first partner that their spouse is
indeed an impossible and threatening person who deserves to be
rejected and hated. All of their dark fantasies and paranoid expectations are given credence. At this point verbal and physical conflict
may escalate, at times unbearably. The contention may continue
until both parties are exhausted. Then they retreat for a time to lick
their wounds. They become "married singles," avoiding each other
as much as possible—at least until the next confrontation.

Initially, divorce may seem to be the obvious solution for the
person who has the allergic reaction, and who will in fact think
about it continually, as a kind of fantasy escape from the irrational
anger and intense irritation toward their partner.

However, in my experience, divorce is usually not the best solution. Because after the romance cools in the *next* marriage, these
very same hidden demons can be reactivated during the normal
stress of adjusting to the new partner. Nothing really changes. In
fact, things could be much worse in the second marriage with the
added complication of mixing "my, his, and our" children, plus the
frequent interference of ex-spouses, not to mention escalating
money problems. Also, many of the positive qualities found in
one's first spouse may be missing in a new mate. Too often I see
people go from the frying pan into the food blender as they flee
one marriage and go into the next with even greater misery.

If only one partner in a marriage has an allergy problem, the
situation is probably curable. But there still will be a price to pay.
It won't be easy. If both have it, the cure rate is much lower, and
the help of an extremely competent therapist is nearly always required.

What If You Are the Rejected One?

If you are the rejected partner whom your spouse can't stand, you must consider that he or she is unwittingly projecting on you dark, ugly fantasies from the past. You are now the hated older brother, parent, or even ex-spouse whom they are reacting to so negatively. You are going to have to develop some compassion, some objectivity, some capacity to forgive them for the venom they are inflicting on you. In one sense you are a partly innocent bystander who is absorbing poisons originating in your spouse's past life. If you are without children, divorce might seem the simpler way out. But remember—whomever else you marry may also have similar demons that will need to be exorcised too.

If you choose to stay, you must realize that for a period of time you will need to do things that will not be easy or seem fair. Equity will be temporarily denied, and you will be giving to the relationship far more than would ordinarily be expected. It will involve some sacrifice. And for a while you may get little but coldness and rejection in return.

Solution Strategies

What does one do? Like physical illnesses, psychological allergies run a course. Eventually your partner may pull out of it (a spontaneous remission), if you don't feed it by engaging in repetitive counterattacks, which would be like pouring gasoline on a fire.

One caution: the suggestions given here apply *only* when your spouse has a true allergy and is *not* involved in an extramarital affair (where their obnoxious or indifferent behavior is a defense, a result of trying to justify their infidelity). Their typical unsound thinking is: "Since I never did really love my spouse [not true]—and I can't stand them anyway—it's okay to love someone else. God will understand!"

And, if indeed, they are involved with someone else, this needs to be confronted directly and quickly. Secrets kill you both. Quickly get it out in the open. This will take a lot of the excitement out of their illicit liaison.

Next you need to decide, despite their problem, if their inner core is basically healthy and decent, worth waiting for, worth re-habilitating. But the most important thing to do—if it is a true al-lergy—is to give them space!

What if they were in the middle of a PMS episode or had a high job stress situation that rendered them difficult and obnoxious? You would back off and let their "illness" take its course, because there is really not a lot that you can do about it. You would know that while they were indisposed, rational dialogue would get you nowhere. It's not your responsibility to fix everything instantly. So relax. Take it easy for a while. It's as if you were saying, "It's okay not to like each other every day in every way. Sometimes I feel ornery and can't stand you either. But I'm certainly not going to lose sleep over it."

This kind of attitude instantly frees you up. It facilitates the healing process. What you are doing is giving them permission to find their way back—for a brief period of time. And remember—someday you may wish them to return the favor. Maybe they have already.

Since they are going to be temporarily out of commission, you need in the meantime to fill your life with other challenges and ex-citing and fulfilling activities. You are not going to stay stuck in a rut with them. Your choice is to move on during that period while they are working through their problems.

Thus you refuse to fight with them. You don't criticize, be-cause it won't do the slightest good. In fact, you can take consider-able pleasure in being helpful, sweet, and reasonable. It will con-fuse them in a helpful and healing way. It also helps a lot not to defend yourself nor repeatedly justify your behavior (because this won't help either).

I must warn you that it will take anywhere from two or three to eighteen months for a change to occur if you follow these guide-lines. I think that how long the allergy lasts depends not only on how you handle it but also on how severe and long-term their prob-lem was with those persons in the past whom they are attacking and rejecting through you. But remember, the key to solving their allergic reaction to you is to give them space, back off, and in the meantime fill your life with positive experiences while staying out of battle. Be noncontentious and Ghandi-like. But I would, in the meantime, certainly consider joining a twelve-step support group focusing on such things as co-dependence and relationships. With a spouse out of commission, you need some nurturing and a safe place. These are free. Pick a group that fits your values and style.

Also don't keep brooding about all of the unfair things your partner is doing. Focus only on what *you can do* to be responsible and attend to your own business. You can never force a partner to love you. But you, yourself, can choose to love. You, by a conscious choice, can be responsible, caring, and loyal, returning anger or rejection with "good gifts." In other words, you can choose *your* behavior. I believe that love is a daily decision. You can choose to love, even though your spouse is temporarily out of commission. Remember, your spouse is damaged for reasons not entirely their fault. They are confused too about why they feel so negatively about you—especially when you have been so kind and reasonable (we hope).

There is a verse in the Bible which suggests that bread cast upon the waters always returns manyfold to the giver (see Ecclesiastes 11:1). I have found this can be particularly true in marital relationships.

In saying all of the above, I do not mean to imply in any way that a wife or husband should tolerate continuing, serious physical or emotional abuse. This is not healthy for either of the spouses nor the children who may witness it. Marital violence is unacceptable and should not be tolerated. If you can't stop it, get ecclesiastical and/or professional help. (Also, see chapter 14, which deals with this issue.)

What If You Are the Offending Party?

What do you do if you are the one who can't stand your spouse?

Even though you may not be able to change your negative *feelings* toward your spouse, you can change your *behavior.* If you are caught in a conflict between your negative feelings and the rational side of your nature (which argues the other way), consider that you are not fully responsible for your reactions and feelings. They originate in your past. They represent inappropriate responses to your partner stemming from previous traumas—similar to phobias, like having an inordinate fear of animals, open spaces, or elevators. However, even though you may not be responsible for their presence, you are responsible for doing something about them now. Remember that a divorce is usually not the best solution and doesn't guarantee that these problems won't show up in future relationships. You might as well deal with them now. You can't run away from yourself or the negative programming that may be within you.

But what else do you do? If you are involved in an extramarital affair, you must realize that it's nearly impossible to cure an "allergy" and handle an affair at the same time. It just won't work: affairs always feed allergies and make them worse.

If there is no affair or the affair is really over (no longing for the other party), then start (this will startle you) *serving* the spouse whom you can't stand. *Give to them!* This needs to be for months, *not just* a day or two. If you are the husband, help more with the dishes and kids. Reduce her stress in a thousand ways! If you are the wife, be more sexually affectionate, noncritical, and helpful.

An important psychological rule is that your *behavior* has to change before your *feelings* will change. Don't worry about the discrepancy in the beginning. It's impossible to really serve somebody and *not* have your heart softened or begin to care and feel for them emotionally. But, again, your behavior change will always precede the change in your feelings. And it has to be totally your free choice to do this to accomplish a good end. This works, but you need to keep it up!

It's like giving to our children. The more we give of ourselves, the more we love them regardless of their sometimes obnoxious, selfish natures. But if you do it, it must be done freely and consciously. It cannot be forced or demanded. In a sense what I am suggesting again is that love is best expressed by action, doing, behavior. It's a decision, but it's a decision that needs to be made every day.

You Have the Power to Change

For the most part you can have almost anything you want in your marriage. I believe there are few accidents in this life. I'm convinced that we create most of our own luck as well as our own joy or misery. In the end we get what we really, consciously or unconsciously, want. It's a fantasy to believe that if only we were married to the right person, life would be great. Most people already are married to the right person but just don't know it. But the *right* person will never be the *perfect* person. That exists only in fiction. Making your relationship great is something you have to make happen. It's your responsibility. If you don't believe this is possible, it isn't. If, however, you believe that you can pull it off, you probably can.

It has to do ultimately with the vision you have for your marriage. It's not something you wait around to see somehow happen. You have to organize events and priorities in order to bring it about. You are not a hapless pawn. You are or can be a master creator. And God will help you if what you want is good.

CHAPTER 20

Premenstrual Syndrome:
Some Days Can Be Tough

Many marriages are stressed, and some have floundered when wives afflicted with premenstrual syndrome (or PMS) become impossible at certain times of the month. A few beat their children, attack their husbands, wreck their cars—just lose control, even in nonprovocative situations—to the distress of all those who live with them.

Barbara, a patient of Katharina Dalton, a prominent British physician and PMS expert, comments: "I have such drastic changes in personality before a period, I think I am going mad. I cannot understand how I can feel so differently toward my children, one day loving and caring for them and the next day hateful and rough, so bad-tempered, smacking them for nothing. I feel so guilty when I see my own daughter, aged five, copying me and smacking her dolls."

Queen Victoria had PMS too. At certain times of the month she would go berserk. She would assault her husband, Albert, with a fury that was totally beyond his comprehension.

A patient at Arizona's Phoenix PMS Institute explained: "There are two me's. For part of the month I am like a raging storm—out of control, hateful to those I love, irritable, depressed, and unlovable. I want to lock myself away, ashamed to inflict myself on anyone. Yet once my period starts the storm calms, and I become the person I like—cheerful, patient, loving and capable."

Over one hundred symptoms are associated with PMS. No one has them all. But a few typical ones include the following:

abdominal bloating	leg cramps	confusion	edema
abdominal cramps	incoordination	rages	fatigue
craving for sweets	breast swelling	fear	diarrhea
breast tenderness	panic	insecurity	anger
backache	itching	epilepsy	headaches
change in sex drive	weakness	asthma	depression
bruising	insomnia	salt craving	irritability
food binges	fainting	aggression	hives

On occasion a woman may even become suicidal or at least accident prone, engage in child abuse, or threaten her marriage.

Although some months will be worse than others, it is important to emphasize that no woman will ever have all of these symptoms, no matter how acute her case is. But the ones she does have can make life difficult for herself and those who live with and love her.

The critical key to diagnosing PMS is not so much *what* symptoms you have but rather that they are showing up on a predictable cyclic basis just prior to menstruation. So chart them for three months on your calendar daily at home. Then discuss your findings with your physician.

PMS Origins

The best evidence suggests that PMS is inherited. Mothers, warn your daughters. While we don't know exactly how this all happens, PMS appears to originate in the hypothalamic pituitary axis of the brain—not in the reproductive organs. Thus, a hysterectomy may make symptoms worse instead of better.

PMS is a combination of physical, behavioral, and emotional symptoms triggered by endocrine changes within the woman's body, occurring on a near-monthly cycle in conjunction with menstruation.

In other words, it is not the woman's fault. No more than an allergy, or blue eyes, or diabetes. But she still has to deal with it and find some kind of relief or else face disturbed relationships in her family, feelings of guilt, and lowered self-esteem.

It's incorrect to equate menstrual cramps with PMS. Menstrual cramps can occur both with or without PMS.

PMS tends to get worse over time if untreated. Typically when it first starts the woman will have a few symptoms a few days prior to her period, which will cease when the period actually starts. Over time the symptoms will start showing up earlier—maybe one or two weeks before menses. With some women there may come a day when there no longer is a clear pattern of good and bad days— just PMS all the time.

What Triggers the First Onset of PMS?

Typically PMS may be triggered by an event such as the birth of a child, a tubal ligation, a hysterectomy, going on or off birth control pills, the onset of menstruation in early puberty, approach of menopause, a life crisis or major trauma such as a death in the family, after a time of no periods (amenorrhea). It can get worse with increasing age, with the use of tranquilizers, or acute stress.

Course of Treatment

The first necessary thing before treatment is to correctly diagnose PMS. Many other illnesses or conditions can present PMS-like symptoms such as a thyroid disorder, neuroses, infections, tumors, psychoses, and ordinary mood swings. It is also possible to have PMS concurrently with some other illnesses, which may complicate matters in diagnosing it.

But the essential key diagnostic indicator of PMS is the repeated cyclic presence of some of the symptoms noted earlier— with a symptom-free period following menstruation.

While figures vary somewhat, D. C. Hammond, a clinical psychologist at the University of Utah medical school who has researched this illness, estimates that 40 percent of adult women experience moderate symptoms of PMS, while another 5 to 10 percent will experience it severely.

For wives who have severe cases of PMS, the social and psychological consequences can be devastating. The condition can severely stress not only the marriage but also the mother's relationship with her children, as well as with neighbors, acquaintances, and people she works with. She can become depressed and feel guilt-ridden because she has so hurt the very people she loves and cares about the most. And in some instances she may not be able to go to work, handle social obligations, or deal with the mildest stresses in her home and family.

In seeking medical help for this condition, you might consider either selecting a physician who has special knowledge about PMS and at least part of his or her practice is devoted to treating this condition. Or if you are in a larger community you might seek out a PMS clinic staffed by knowledgeable physicians, nurses, psychologists, nutritionists, and other appropriate specialists. Such clinics often put women with PMS into support groups where they are able to share their experiences and learn more about diet or other things that can ameliorate their illness.

Joseph Martorano, M.D., president of the PMS Medical Group in New York City, believes, as does Katharina Dalton, M.D., that PMS sufferers have a relative deficiency of the hormone progesterone.

In the normal woman, progesterone acts as a natural diuretic, which serves to keep water from accumulating in the body's tissues. Dr. Martorano points out that if progesterone levels are deficient, the body retains excess water and salt, producing bloat, tension, fatigue, joint pain, and weight gain. But more important, a progesterone deficiency interferes with the body's ability to metabolize sugar, resulting in hypoglycemia, or low blood sugar. And this is where we get the symptoms which include headaches, fainting, weakness, irritability, rage, even panic.

Since birth-control pills have *progestogens*, a synthetic version of progesterone, some physicians and patients have felt the pill would also help control the PMS problem, but because its chemical makeup is somewhat different, it just so happens that the synthetic progestogens act to *drive down* the level of a woman's natural progesterone. This of course can accentuate PMS symptoms. Thus, oral contraceptives can actually aggravate the problem for some PMS sufferers. Natural progesterone appears to be a safe hormone, not linked to cancer as is estrogen in a few women. In fact, during pregnancy the body increases progesterone production by fifteen times the normal rate, which is probably why PMS symptoms usually do not occur during pregnancy.

At the Utah PMS Center in Salt Lake City, which has seen over two thousand patients, about 80 percent of the women respond favorably to natural progesterone, but many physicians and health care workers feel that other strategies are needed also. Thus some women also benefit from a combination of antidepressant medications and psychotherapy.

Natural progesterone and a hypoglycemia-type diet are both extremely helpful in treating this illness. The recommended diet (starting several days before symptoms appear) is six small meals a day, or three moderate meals plus three snacks between meals, with absolutely no fasting or skipping meals. These meals should emphasize complex carbohydrates and high-protein foods, since these break down more slowly in the body. This diet results in a more constant stream of sugar into the blood. Whole grains and green leafy vegetables are also recommended as part of the diet.

Sugar, fats, caffeine (chocolate, colas, and coffee) and alcohol should be either sharply restricted or eliminated at this time, since their intake can have an almost immediate negative effect on blood-sugar levels. If there is a water-retention problem (bloating), salt must also be curtailed. Getting daily exercise (aerobics, swimming, jogging, etc.) plus adequate rest (to reduce stress) may also relieve symptoms.

Also recommended are daily multivitamin-mineral supplements, especially including C, the B complex, magnesium, calcium, phosphorous, and zinc.

Christiane Northrup, M.D., in her excellent book *Women's Bodies, Women's Wisdom,* also recommends consumption of the essential fatty acids (especially linoleic acid) for proper metabolism of hormones. These essential fatty acids can also be found in raw nuts and seeds or evening primrose oil. She also mentions that sufficient exposure to natural light is helpful. She notes that inadequate exposure to light is associated with the illness SAD (seasonal affective disorder) with many symptoms identical to PMS. Light acts as a nutrient. It directly influences the entire neuroendocrine system through the retina, the hypothalamus, and pineal gland. So expose yourself several hours a day to full spectrum light or natural sunlight. Research documents its healing power (e.g., B.L. Barry et. al., *American Journal of Psychiatry*, vol. 146, 1991, p. 9).

To summarize, you can do seven important things with the assistance of a competent physician or PMS clinic to alleviate your problems with PMS:

1. Prior to the appearance of the symptoms, go on a hypoglycemia diet (six small meals or snacks, high complex carbohydrate food, low fat, low sugar, no caffeine—as in colas, chocolate, or coffee).

2. Under the direction of a physician who is a specialist in this area, start natural progesterone a day or two before your usual monthly symptoms show up. It is usually prescribed in vaginal or rectal-suppository form but can also be given by intramuscular injection or rectally in fluid form.

3. Exercise daily (brisk walking, any aerobics, etc.), get sufficient rest, and engage in other stress-reduction techniques.

4. Try a multivitamin-mineral complex that includes the B complex (especially B-3 and B-6), C, magnesium, phosphorous, zinc, and calcium; as well as linoleic acid. While the evidence isn't complete on exactly how these work, some PMS clinics have found them helpful with their patients.

5. Consider joining a PMS support group. Call your local PMS clinic or physician for directions on how to make contact with such a group.

6. If your marriage has been acutely stressed by your PMS, get involved in couples therapy or a marriage enrichment program. When in therapy, focus some attention on anger control and conflict resolution.

7. Get exposure to full spectrum light (two hours a day, 2500 lux or more). This could in part be natural sunlight during your exercise time if outside.

All of the above strategies have been helpful for *some* PMS women. Some of these you can do on your own. Others will require the support and direction of health care professionals. This is an immensely complex illness with much variation in its expression from woman to woman. What approaches will help with some may not make a big difference with others. As you go through the healing journey, listen to the language of your body: it will tell you what is right for you.

Menopausal Symptoms

In the case of menopausal symptoms, not all related to PMS, which can also stress a marriage, I have found the following to help: (1) hormone replacement therapy prescribed by a highly competent gynecologist; (2) working in a positive job situation; (3) good nutrition, vitamins, and exercise; (4) involvement in nurturing support groups (church, social organizations, clubs); (5) interesting hobbies; and (6) personal therapy, as needed.

PART 3

When Divorce Is the Only Way

CHAPTER 21

Deciding on Divorce: Should I Stay and Suffer or Leave and Die?

I want out! I've had it! This is it!" has perhaps been uttered at one time or another by every husband and wife who ever lived, even in the very best marriages.

The question is, when is this for real? When does one really follow through—or when *should* one follow through?

How much pain should one endure before throwing in the towel? How bad does your partner have to be before you give them the ax?

Since the consequences of divorce can be devastating to one's emotional health, as well as standard of living—not to mention its impact on the children—this is one decision that should be given the utmost consideration.

Three Key Rules in Deciding About Divorce

First: Don't Threaten. In my judgment, you should not threaten your spouse with divorce. That gives them negative expectations. In time you may program them to *expect* divorce. Then they may start acting as if it were about to happen. If you keep threatening, they may call your bluff and move out of the relationship, possibly becoming interested in someone else *because they believe you*. Thus, you may find that you will have to go through with something you are not really certain you want to do. You will have painted yourself into a corner.

I see too many people faced with *solvable* problems in relatively good marriages who are still getting divorced. It is a terrible waste because, in many cases, the next marriage or relationship is not only no better, it may be much worse. And this is an awful trade!

Second: Consider the Most Important Issue—Willingness to Change. I do not see infidelity, spouse abuse, lack of affection, noncommunication, stinginess, little time together, or a drinking problem as being necessary grounds for divorce. The more important issue is: Can your spouse change? Can you change? Do either of you *want* to change? Again, every wife (including mine) has grounds for divorce. But so does every husband.

There is pain at times in every relationship. And sometimes that pain is almost more than one can bear. But a doctor doesn't shoot his patients as a solution to their being ill. And most parents don't trade in their kids just because they won't mind them. No! They handle it! They solve the problem. And, of course, most of us don't get divorced just because we have difficulties in our relationship. Even if one of the marital pair is balky and somewhat uncooperative, the other, alone, can still make significant changes which can improve the climate of the whole marriage.

Third: Look at the Inner Core. Problems we have with our spouses are often due to inappropriate prior learning, a damaged upbringing, or even a messed-up prior marriage. Like pups who mess in the front room, some spouses are not fully "housebroken" yet. They may be still immature and selfish, or they may be operating on the basis of false beliefs (e.g., "All women flirt," or "Someone else will always pay the bill").

So when we carefully look at our flawed partner we need to ask, What is the nature of their basic inner core? Is he or she worth waiting for, fighting for? If they were healed, if they grew up, if they were rehabilitated, could I love what remained—the true inner core of their personality? The truth is that there are many truly great people who are diamonds in the rough, who *are* worth waiting for. Is my spouse one of these?

While some individuals believe that you ought to stay in an awful marriage "for the sake of the kids," no matter what the cost or pain, I do not always agree. It is not doing the children a favor to stay in an extremely destructive marriage that has little hope of change. It is better for children to have one stable parent than to live in the continuing hell of acute marital stress that devastates both parents and children alike.

A *Checklist to Rate Your Spouse and Marriage*

I would next like to suggest a checklist you might review before making the decision whether to stay in and salvage your present marriage.

1. If your spouse has a major mental illness, the longer he or she has had it and the more serious it is, the less chance there is for change. This includes sexual deviations, alcoholism, psychosis, or long-standing serious neurotic hang-ups. The key issues are: Are they getting better or worse? How is it affecting the children? Is your partner willing to get professional help? And to what extent can you live with it?

2. If your spouse has had an affair, the key issues here are: Is this a lifelong compulsive pattern or an isolated event? Is this a major emotional involvement or a one-time sexual experience? If they wish to return to the marriage, can you forgive them? Can you wait until the involvement ends? Sometimes it is not all that easy to instantly turn off one's affection for another person. Is it possible to improve your relationship, negotiate solutions, and renew trust?

3. If you have a major communication problem, would your spouse be willing to participate in special workshops

or get professional help that might improve your skills in this area?

4. Would your spouse be willing to see a marriage counselor? And if the first did not work out, would you both be willing to try another one or two until one is found who is right for your situation?

5. Are there interfering in-laws? If so, would your spouse be willing to deal with their destructive influence or even, as a possibility, move to a new area?

6. In the case of spouse abuse (physical or verbal), is this a lifelong pattern of violence or just a rare outburst at a time of considerable stress? Is he or she willing to get help?

7. In nearly all cases sexual incompatibility can be treated by competent therapists. Would you and your spouse be willing to get counseling from a therapist, choosing someone you both could relate to and be comfortable with?

8. In the case of conflict in values (including different preferences in friends, religion, politics, use of drugs, etc.), the big issue is whether you can remain with a spouse who philosophically lives in a different world or who rejects your set of basic beliefs. I find that this is an area where people really do not change much. Can you accept your spouse for what he or she is, especially considering their impact on your growing children? And can your spouse accept *you?*

9. Are money problems a temporary issue in your marriage, or is your spouse unable to contribute significant economic support to the family? Can you live with this if it does not change much from the pattern of the last five years?

10. Does your spouse have the capacity to change? Look at your history together to determine the answer to this. Does

your spouse have the *desire and commitment* to change? It is deeds, not words, that count here. If they do not change, what will it be like ten years from now for you and your children? Can you live with this?

11. How destructive or inadequate are your spouse's parenting skills? How damaging is her or his impact on the children? Is your spouse willing to change, to get help? Can your spouse change even if given help? Has your spouse changed for the better at any time in the past? What positive contributions does your spouse make to the children now?

Are Marriage Counselors Worth It? How Do You Find One?

Our research clearly indicates that some marriage counselors are disasters. They tend to create problems, not solve them. But there are some who are extraordinarily skillful in helping couples resolve their conflicts. In my experience, this has nothing to do with their profession, sex, or age. Also, a particular therapist may have an outstanding reputation but for a particular couple may prove unsuitable. So what do you do? Check around with friends, family, a physician, an ecclesiastical leader, and anyone you know in the mental health field. I would suggest going at least twice to the best therapist on your list. If the chemistry somehow does not work or you are just not satisfied, tactfully cancel your next appointment and see another counselor. You should feel no guilt over doing this. It is your marriage, your future, that's at stake.

It is better that both of you work with the same therapist, because the counselor will know both sides of the story and also get continuing feedback on whether you are doing your homework. This makes it nearly impossible for either partner to lie or fake it. The single counselor can keep you both responsible. I believe it is a high risk to see separate therapists for primarily marital problems, because neither counselor will ever know the whole truth about the relationship and be able to give you the best advice.

I have repeatedly had the experience, after hearing a wife tell a tale of woe about a man who did not know how to love her properly or who abused her for many years, of wiping a tear or two away with my handkerchief and wondering how she ever put up with the bum. But after listening to her husband's story (which I always insist on hearing if I am to help the couple), I again have my handkerchief out wondering how he ever endured all those years of misery living with her. Sometimes the tale is so sad I use two handkerchiefs.

The striking differences between the two stories are almost universal, even when both are being truthful. It is just that they each leave out certain important things. Good counseling is impossible unless the counselor has a chance of finding the truth by hearing both spouses' versions of it.

In addition to help from a really good therapist, I recommend (as previously mentioned) that couples struggling to overcome communication blocks take part in such valuable experiences as evening classes on marriage or communication, or community seminars, such as David Mace's Marriage Enrichment seminars.* Or you might consider the Marriage Encounter weekend seminars. These are sponsored by various religious groups (Catholics, Lutherans, Presbyterians, Jews, Episcopalians) who welcome non-member couples. These are all very safe but powerful experiences given at a very reasonable cost. Couples are treated lovingly with no real possibility of embarrassment or abrasive confrontations. The dignity and privacy of the couple are always fully respected.

I believe that it is possible for most mismatched couples to make it if both put energy and inspiration into their relationship. I also believe that two quite well matched and highly compatible people can divorce if they fail to nurture their relationship. What I am suggesting is that you are not a helpless pawn who has little or no control over your destiny. Divorce doesn't just happen—you choose it. But in many, maybe most, cases, you can choose to stay in your marriage and make dramatic changes. There will be some stress and pain that way. But divorce will also extract its "pound of flesh." You have the choice.

---

*Write ACME for details, Box 10596, Winston-Salem, North Carolina 27108.

CHAPTER 22

Choosing the
Right One

Let's say you are divorced. It was a miserable experience. And you are now ready to try again. Or maybe you find yourself thirty and still looking, and there's nothing but frogs and flakes out there. No prince or princess—at least in *your* office.

You want somebody you can respect, who's interesting, warm, and affectionate. But who is also responsible—not a doper, or gay, or not quite sure what they are. Somebody you can trust, who has some integrity, who won't pull the rug out from under you. Where do you find quality people like that? Especially somebody who matches your personality and would not be afraid to make a commitment if the chemistry were right.

I can assure you that there *are* indeed many quality single people out there of both sexes! I see and meet with them all the time. Something like a third of all adults in our society are single, and a good portion of these are quality. And with the exception of those who are gay, most are looking to connect with someone wonderful of the opposite sex.

One of the main reasons many singles are not married and still looking is fear: fear of being hurt again, fear of commitment, and doubts about their judgment. Other reasons include poor social skills or limited opportunity—not being in circles where they can meet suitable partners. Many of these people are diamonds in the rough who have been passed over because they may not have a high gloss of self-confidence. Yet they are good people and in all likelihood would probably make excellent spouses.

Too Few Available Men?

Many young women get psyched out when reading the statistics on the shortage of available men on the singles' scene. As you increase in age, especially as you move into and beyond your thirties this disparity does get greater. But so what? The same thing is true in the job market. There is always competition for the really good positions. However, if your intention is clear, your energy focused, and you go after it you can have nearly anything you want.

Why is this so? Because there are so many other people out there—an incredible number—who have mixed and confused motivation about marriage, job hunting, or any other major life enterprise. They are not even in the race! They are not really seriously looking. They are standing on the sidelines. Many are apathetic and immobilized. If they do end up in the winner's circle, which of course a few of them do, it's usually only accidental. Your competition is not really that great. There are so many out there who think that it's not really possible to reach their goal. Guess what? It's true for them. So they aren't even trying. But that need not be so for you.

I see people even in their eighties finding a special someone and saying their "I do's." Regardless of your age or situation, nearly anything is possible for you *if* you are really willing to go for it and are not afraid. But you have got to be willing to pay the price and have the energy to make it happen.

It's Okay to Be Attractive

If you are truly interested in finding a partner I think that it's important that you "package yourself" attractively. This may be old hat to you, but it still is important and needs to be said again and still again. If you want to "make it" socially and find someone very special, you've got to like yourself enough to dress well and look sharp. I see some singles who look as if they had been out-fitted by a second-hand clothing store.

Some of us do not have a particularly strong style or color sense, but despite that it is still possible to look great. Many of us need a little help. So, find a "consultant"—someone with exceptional taste in this area. If they let me decorate the interior of my home it would look like a Greyhound bus depot—a disaster, in other words. So I have the good sense to let others do most of it. Do whatever you have to do, so that if you are a woman, your hair has a terrific cut. Get the best. Don't compromise. Have it shaped to fit your face and figure. Next, your wardrobe—you don't need a full closet. But what you do get should look really great on you, even your grubbies! This applies to men too. Whenever you wear clothes that look exceptionally attractive on you, it elevates your spirit and actually makes you feel great inside—and you will have more bounce and vitality, feeling invigorated as you notice all the admiring glances.

Most large cities have one or two extra-classy department stores that may be on the expensive side but which take great pains to sell quality clothing. Most have a special staff of clothing consultants (not the regular clerks), well trained with excellent taste, who will assist you at no charge in picking out an attractive wardrobe or individual items of clothing that will look great on you. Check them out and see what they recommend specifically for you. You are not obligated to buy anything, even though they hope that you eventually will. Take along a friend whose judgment you value and get their reaction too.

I'm Single, Female, and Overweight— What Do You Recommend?

Have you ever noticed how many happily *married* women are also overweight? Somebody found *them* attractive and fell in love with *them* at some time. It is important not to let weight become an obsession for you, because this can actually work against you in shedding pounds. However, it is still wise, for health considerations as well as aesthetic reasons, to maintain control over your weight. But you don't have to be a fanatic about it!

The two major approaches to weight control involve exercise and diet. In my experience, exercise takes only a moderate amount of weight off but it can help most in redistributing it so that you can look really good: firm and trim even though you may still be over your desired weight level. However, a *limited but nutritious diet over a period of time* is the thing that really takes the pounds off.

As I have worked with people who have lost weight, I have found that each had to find their own system. There is not one best way. Weight Watchers helps a lot of people but not all. Others ask friends and acquaintances for recommendations of weight-loss programs that have helped them take off weight, and keep it off.

What is critical is avoiding such booby traps as wedding receptions, parties, holidays, and overly sumptuous dinner dates. The successful way to handle those occasions with all of their tempting calories is to *plan your strategy in advance.* Figure out ahead of time exactly how you will say no and avoid the tempting goodies. Visualize in detail how you will handle it—successfully. At some social events you might carry around a half-full glass of ice and water (or soda water) all night. With your hand occupied people are less likely to push food and high-calorie drinks at you.

With some people, eating high-calorie junk food is an addiction—a little like the alcoholic's. I'm convinced that having a support group of other heavies who are committed to weight control and overcoming this mutual problem can be a major help. Why not organize such a group yourself and meet weekly? It helps to have to be responsible to other caring people in resisting temptation. Alcoholics Anonymous uses group support with tremendous success. Examine their strategies and employ them with appropriate modifications in the group you put together.

The Fitness Factor

While taking a break at a vacation resort recently, I went to several physical fitness and diet lectures. The instructor, a very attractive woman in her late twenties, looked absolutely great. Her posture and bearing were confident and dynamic. Her eyes were full of sparkle and vitality. Her body appeared trim and lean. Not the slightest bulge at midriff. Just beautifully packaged. At the end of the lecture she mentioned that she was five feet seven inches and asked us to guess her weight.

Nobody came close. When she mentioned 150 pounds several women in the audience shrieked in disbelief. In fact, one jumped up and stood beside her, comparing bodies and announcing, "But I weigh only 142 and look how dumpy I am. I look terrible and you look fantastic. It's not fair!" And indeed this woman did look like an oversized bag of potatoes. She was dumpy at less weight, while the fitness instructor looked more like a perfect ten.

It is possible to get so obsessed by your actual poundage that you forget about the general shape and tone of your whole body. You don't have to be skinny to look great. But you do have to work at taking care of yourself; do aerobics, stretching, and other exercises on a regular basis.

There is no doubt that some individuals inherit a large frame or tendencies to put on weight easily, while others can eat like sin and still look fairly decent. It is genetically programmed within them. All this means is that some people will have to focus more time and energy on weight control than others. You may not think this is fair, but skinny people have other kinds of problems and challenges. These kinds of things, I've found, all seem to balance out in life.

Wanda's Solution

One day Wanda entered my office. She had a gorgeous face but carried 220 heavy pounds on her frame. Her personality was very engaging. She had the prettiest smile. She had been briefly married in her late teens. She was now twenty-seven and felt very blue about her lack of social life. She had fought the weight battle for well over a decade—always losing. Diet programs—you name them, she had tried them all. On several occasions she had taken off as much as forty pounds. But it never lasted. She just didn't have the self-discipline to do what needed to be done in a consistent, long-term way.

We counseled together about many issues on and off for many months. But the weight problem never really changed. Then one day I told her that I had known a married woman with a sizable family who had struggled with a weight problem for years and finally decided to have a "stomach staple" operation. She lost her weight and now has the physique of a college student. In this major operation, the size of the stomach is surgically reduced so that only small amounts of food can be eaten at one time. This leads, in time, to substantial and permanent weight reduction.

After much consideration Wanda decided to do the same. She chose an excellent surgeon who had a good reputation with this operation with many successful outcomes. She did not reveal to anyone outside her family the exact nature of or reason for the surgery. She was just a little embarrassed about it all. Her physician indicated that there would be some digestive discomfort and nausea as her body adjusted to this radical change in the way it processed food. And, certainly, the way she would handle meals in the future would change. In any event the operation was very successful. She lost her weight and looked very svelte and attractive. And this was relatively permanent. She bought a new wardrobe and started dating. Within a year she married—happily—and now has her first child. Five years later saw modest weight gain.

While this represented a rather radical solution for Wanda, she did what she had to do to solve her problem. Her intention was clear. She was prepared to make whatever sacrifices needed to be made. I do not mean to recommend this radical kind of approach for solving every weight problem. In fact, some operations don't work out that successfully. All I am suggesting is that you handle the problem—any way it will work for you. But handle it!

My Opera Star

Several years ago a young opera singer came in for counseling with a unique problem. She had three handsome suitors asking for her hand in marriage. She wanted to get married, but was not sure which young man was the most suitable. Each had some very strong points, but these were quite different for each man. One was very intelligent but a little on the serious side; another was extremely engaging socially and had a winning sense of humor but was not always as responsible as he might be; the third was very ambitious and successful financially but was not always gracious.

Her goal in counseling was to find out how she might make the best decision. Which one should she marry? Needless to say, I was not foolish enough to make that selection for her. That had to remain her choice. Subsequent events proved she made a good decision. Her marriage has turned out very well. But, at the time, it was a very trying experience for her. In fact, one solution she seriously but only briefly considered, to escape the stress, was rejecting all three. It would seem that life has a different set of growth experiences in store for each one of us. So our task is to accept responsibility for our own lives—we can't run away—face our special tests squarely and find solutions that we can live with. It's up to us to decide whether to stay stuck or move ahead. As the old saying goes: If it is to be, it's up to me.

How Do You Know for Sure About Someone?

For most unmarried or divorced adults the question will be a little different from that faced by our opera singer. It will be more like, is this person whom I am dating good husband (or wife) material? Dare I let myself fall in love with them? Can I risk it? What will they be like as a parent, a provider or coprovider, as a friend, a lover? Will they "wear well"? Do they have secret hang-ups? Can I trust them? Will they be faithful to me? Am I right for them?

Let me share with you some ideas on how you might predict the future behavior of this special person with whom you are now in a relationship. What I say will also apply to any future relationships you might enter.

First, understand that all of us have special "tapes" or programs in our head that powerfully influence how we handle most life situations. These originate mainly through the experiences we have had growing up in our family and early environment. Thus, the boy who was repeatedly beaten when he disobeyed his father is at risk to repeat this pattern with his own sons, especially when he is under stress. The daughter with the cold, distant father may have greater difficulty relating to men than will the daughter with the warm, affectionate father. They have been programmed to re-late to men in different ways. So what you want to look at is your partner's cross-sex parent relationship. How did your boyfriend get along with his mother (or ex-wife)? How did your girlfriend get along with her father (or ex-husband)?

Also, what kind of role model was her (his) same-sex parent? Then look at how they have related to members of the opposite sex during the last five years. This will be the single most power-ful predictor of how they will do in the next five years in earning income, being responsible, and successfully relating to members of the opposite sex. I do not mean to suggest that people can't change or are 100 percent locked into these patterns—but it's still a factor you need to look at closely.

You should also realize that many people have more than one ego state within their personalities. This means that they can have several identities, only one of which you will usually see when you are first dating them. You might call them "Jekyll and Hyde" types.

When Sandra, twenty-five, was engaged to Karl, she found him to be the kindest, most generous person she had ever gone with. He overwhelmed her with gifts and gentle affection. He joined her religion. Theirs was an ideal courtship until two months before the wedding. While she was visiting her parents in another state she received a surprise phone call from him. He was ex-tremely quarrelsome, critical, even abusive, haranguing her for an hour over the phone.

She was astonished at this radical departure from his previous demeanor. She had never seen this side of him before. She wept many bitter tears and went into a period of confusion and depres-sion. Several days later he called back and apologized profusely. He was now his sweet old gentle self. Gradually, as he alternated between abuse and gentleness, she recognized that he had virtu-ally two different identities within his personality. Faced with such unpredictable behavior, she finally terminated the engagement.

It is important to know your partner long enough and see them under a variety of life stresses and in many different situations. You should also talk with friends who have known them for many years, for, as previously mentioned, their past five years' behavior will be the most accurate predictor that we have of future behavior in or out of the marriage. This is not to suggest that having several ego states is all bad; it isn't. But if you are going to entrust your life and the lives of your children to someone else, you want to know ahead of time what you are getting into so that you can make an informed decision.

Differences in Values and Ultimate Goals

Olive was a child of the hippie generation, and Fred was an elitist, Ivy League banker. She was a flaky drug user and a fantastic sexual partner. But he could not trust her for more than five seconds with pills, booze, or other men. She was always looking for the ultimate turn-on. Her motto was "Do it!" regardless of what "it" was.

Undeniably, their chemistry was exceptional. But their core values were light years apart. She hated his prissy Protestant ethic and obsessive need to keep their bank account balanced. Revolting! She saw him as a stuffy and unspontaneous gray flannel suit with a damnable inner compulsion for neatness, order, and certainty.

Not only that, but he believed in God and prayed nightly. She believed in cocaine and multiple orgasms. These were her gods, and she worshipped them regularly. He thought he could tame her, maybe even save her. He saw himself as the needed balance in her life. She saw marriage as something to be tried and maybe savored. If it worked, fine. If it didn't, who cares—she'd move on.

In my experience couples who have major goal and value conflicts or radical differences in lifestyles almost never make it in marriage. The only exception to this is where one partner changes or is converted over to the other's view. If you are in a relationship where there are profound value differences, the issue you are faced with is, can you handle it—especially when children are involved? Because no matter what you do, some of the kids will identify with and assume some of the traits and values of your spouse. Is that acceptable? Are these consequences something you can live with? If you are not sure about your answers to these questions, talk with an unbiased third party, somebody wise and mature, because ten years from now you will not be able to undo the decision you made today. You don't want major regrets down the line.

With Focused Energy and Clear Intention Anything Is Possible

Let me briefly summarize. I am convinced that you can have almost anything you want. But first you need a clear perception of what your goal is, of what you want to create in terms of present and future relationships. Then you need to focus some energy and imagination on meeting enough other singles so that you have a choice. Take evening classes. Join spas or health clubs. Get active in your religious group, volunteer for political work, develop friendship networks with marrieds and singles through whom you can meet attractive people. One college girl I know formed a team of several other singles, each of whom lined the others up with attractive dates of their own choosing. It worked very successfully.

One young woman I know found a husband in two and a half years after she decided to change jobs and residences annually as a way of meeting new people. The new girl in town is always more interesting and exciting than plain Nell who has been working at the same job in the same office for the past five years. Others have been successful by taking self-development seminars, not only to enhance their personality but also to meet other attractive singles.

Make sure you can present yourself with ease and confidence in social interactions; at the same time be realistic about what you want in a partner. What you really want is somebody who complements your personality. Someone whom you can love and who will love you, a person who is stable and responsible, who shares your values and has the flexibility to grow in the relationship. This is the partnership that can become the source of your mutual, renewable joy.

Make a plan. Write it out in detail. Then in a quiet place actually visualize it happening—at least once a day. Get consultation about it. Pray about it. Then work your plan! Remember, if you think your dream is possible, it is. God helps those who help themselves. Especially those who have a clear, positive plan.

CHAPTER 23

Remarriage: Yours, Mine, and Ours (Defusing the Booby Traps)

Many years ago, a marriage-counselor friend of mine lost his wife. He waited until his children were virtually raised before re-marrying. Why? His counseling experience had convinced him that it was almost impossible to blend two families, each with its own separate identity and history, into one successful family. He wouldn't waste his time—and emotions—trying.

I know another man who lost his wife. He had six children. He remarried, and his new wife had no children of her own. They were very much in love, but after some months of marriage the children announced to their father that his new wife was unaccept-able to them. She would have to leave.

She did. At the present time his wife lives in a separate apart-ment where he visits her frequently; his primary home is with the children, until they are grown. He has found this to be the only so-lution that will keep his marriage alive and his family peaceful.

Combining two separate families into one is the most difficult and challenging human experience I know of. These two families solved the problem by sidestepping it, and perhaps that is the safest course—to simply avoid trying. Yet with our soaring divorce rate, it is obvious that there are increasing numbers of single-parent households every year. Is it fair to expect the divorced mother with two or three children to spend the rest of her prime adult years slaving at the office and coming home to work even harder in the incredibly difficult job of raising children without a spouse? Is it reasonable to expect a man or woman who has become used to the interdependence and companionship of marriage—even an unworkable one—to suddenly decide that "for the sake of the children" he or she will forgo that companionship for fifteen or twenty years?

Divorced and widowed parents do have a right to happiness and emotional fulfillment in a sustained love relationship. That right is at least as important as the children's right to have a secure and comfortable home. In fact, the children of a lonely, unfulfilled single parent are likely to have a good share of problems anyway. Yet the addition of a new spouse to a previously established family—particularly when the newcomer brings more children to the home—is as tricky a procedure as a surgical transplant. The possibility of rejection is high; there is a long, difficult period in which the tiniest fluctuations in the family's "health" can be magnified into major crises. At best the experience is trying for everyone. At its worst, the new marriage is destroyed before it is fairly begun.

I have seen many such marriages in serious trouble. Marsha, for instance, came to me in tears. "But Ned and I loved each other so much when we married two years ago. Now he's cold and critical. He had two teenage sons from his previous marriage, and I have my three little ones. It's just hell all the time. His boys are constantly teasing my children, and it's cruel. The little ones are in tears all the time. When I tell Ned about it he won't do a thing— his boys can do no wrong in his view. They're spoiled brats. And when I try to discipline them, they just laugh at me and say, 'Lay off it, old lady; you aren't our mother.'

"They even lie to Ned about me—and he believes *them* instead of *me*. He thinks I'm mean to his sons, unfair to them. *Unfair!* Heaven knows I've tried. I just wish he'd try to like *my* kids. He isn't used to having small children around, I guess. They make him nervous. So my kids don't feel close to him at all."

What Are the Risks in Remarriage?

The remarriage with the lowest risk of failure is the one in which no children are involved. There are possibly still hang-ups, self-doubts, and insecurities left over from a previous marital failure, but unless one of the partners is mentally disturbed, a childless remarriage is workable as long as the partners are reasonably compatible and both want it to work.

The next safest remarriage prospect is when only the wife brings young children into the new family from a previous marriage. She already has a bonded relationship with the children, and since the husband usually works, the wife may have special time at home alone with the children when he is away. Then, when he comes home in the evening, the children aren't as likely to feel threatened when she gives him some attention; they are secure in her love for them.

In such families, it is often best for the husband to take a "nice uncle" role with the children; mother is the primary discipliner. The children won't have a radical change in the family rules with this kind of remarriage. Gradually, if he wants to and does it carefully, with the full support of his wife, the stepfather can establish much closer bonds with the children until a full father-child relationship is formed. Yet even if such a bond is never completely formed, the marriage can be livable, particularly if new children are born who have no reservations about loving both parents fully.

If both parents work, however, the risks increase. The mother has no extra time with the children. Both parents are already tired, and with the demands of children, they may not have the energy and emotional resources to work through the normal posthoneymoon adjustment that all newlyweds seem to need. Also, the time the wife gives her new husband is perceived by the children as time "stolen" from them by this stranger.

An alternative that some single parents have tried is to remain unmarried while attempting to fill their emotional needs through a series of transient relationships. In my counseling experience I have found this usually to be a pretty rocky road. The single parent's emotional needs are not really met—there is no permanence, no commitment, and instead of providing emotional support in the parent's difficult and lonely life, these relationships too often involve strained role playing, deceptions, and brutal letdowns. They often drain far more from the single parent than they give. In time the parent may become very defensive, even paranoid about members of the opposite sex. These relationships, however discreet, always take a toll on the children's security, too. And for men and women in their thirties and forties, the singles' world is often a heartless, cold place to roam.

Sooner or later, most single people with children look for some more permanent kind of union. Despite the risks of remarriage, it looks more attractive than remaining single. If you are contemplating remarriage, is there something you can do to improve your chances of success?

Stacking the Deck in Your Favor

The younger your children are when you remarry, the easier it will be for them to form close emotional bonds with your new spouse. Often when the children are too old, close bonding is simply impossible—and may not even be desirable. A fifteen-year-old girl may not want to call Mom's new husband *Dad*. In her view, he can never be her *real* dad. But the husband *can* become friends with the child, as long as he is careful not to step over the line into the role the child thinks of as *father.* It requires tact, persistence, imagination, and commitment.

As a new stepfather, you should know that having a good relationship with your wife's children will definitely improve the chances of the second marriage succeeding. Do everything possible to create an amicable relationship. Don't demand instant affection or intimacy; simply help the kids associate you with pleasant things. This may require the use of a golf course or, with the younger children, your local version of Disneyland. This is comparable to trying to sell a tough customer in your business by wining and dining him. Play the role of the "good guy" and, especially in the first year of the new marriage, let the child's true parent do most of the "dirty work," the disciplining, though you must remember to give her a great deal of private emotional support.

It doesn't work quite so easily in reverse—when a stepmother is home with this new set of kids while the father, the real parent, is at work. It is especially hard with teenage children. Discipline is tossed into the stepmother's lap by default. What can she do?

As an at-home stepmother, you will initially have to soft-pedal disciplining, except on the most vital issues. First you must become their friend. If they are obnoxious, just think of it as working in an office with a difficult co-worker. Ignore what you can, roll with the punches, and remain polite at all possible costs. Try to do nothing provocative, but there is no law that says you have to like them. If the aggravation becomes too great, it may be necessary for the child to visit the home of the other parent or other relatives for a while. Better this than going through another divorce! To survive, newlywed parents need constant close communication and daily recommitment to each other, as well as frequent breaks away from the kids.

Premarriage Strategy

You should openly discuss ahead of time the fact that joining together your two separate families will sometimes be stressful. You will have to be prepared to actively resist attempts by your children to divide your relationship.

During the courtship period you must court your betrothed's children as well. Bring them gifts, read to the young ones, go on joint outings, talk to them, take them to dinner, and in general develop an active, compatible, friendly relationship. If this is done skillfully, when you marry you will not be seen as a rival. The children will see it as gaining another parent, rather than having to share their true mother or father with you. Everybody wins.

If this isn't handled diplomatically, however, you could easily become the children's enemy. They will only know you as the stranger who always takes Mom or Dad away at night, the interloper who is usurping their true parent's place. It's like having to take a tremendous salary cut in emotional dollars, and they won't like it one bit. It will feel like a *loss*, and I have found that most children tend to be very poor losers. They will attempt to scuttle your new marriage to get even, and kids can, if they want, make great wrecking crews.

If you wait too long to remarry, it can become increasingly difficult for the children to handle. They get used to living with only one parent. It is even harder when some of the younger children are used to sleeping in Mother's bed with her. If this is a pattern of some years' duration, the children will become even more jealous of the new spouse and compete for the real parent's affection and bed. And that bruising parent-child stress will always affect the vital core of the marriage. You will catch yourself thinking like this:

"Was I really fair to my children when I remarried?"

"The poor kids—no wonder they're acting so badly, when I've spent so little time with them lately."

"How can I get mad at them?"

"He's not their *real* father—he just doesn't understand them like I do."

"What right does she have to get so angry at them? They're not her kids—she just doesn't have any patience with them because she doesn't love them."

Before you take the step of getting remarried, you need to face these problems, resolve them, and refuse to doubt each other. Set up some rules and follow them carefully. Some good ones might be:

1. *In an argument between children and the new parent, the real parent will always back up the new parent.* This may seem unfair, but you must realize that any time the children argue with your new spouse, they are really also testing *you*. If your commitment to the new spouse seems weak, it will encourage them just as the scent of blood lures sharks. They will gnaw and nibble all the more. But if they see that you have no intention of giving any ground—if they see that you intend this marriage to be permanent—they will gradually realize that they have much more to lose by fighting with your new spouse than they could possibly gain.

2. *Pity for the children should not excuse their unacceptable behavior.* Don't be fooled—kids can manipulate you more easily through your pity and guilt than through any other

emotion you have! Why do you think babies learn to fake crying or coughing at such an early age? They know it will bring Mommy and Daddy on the run! Once they catch on that crying or eulogizing their missing parent or talking about how "lonely" they are will make their real parent turn into jelly, they'll do it all the time, and your new marriage will founder. Sure, you can't help feeling sorry for them, but it's like the man on trial for murdering his parents. Should the jury be moved when the lawyer pleads, "But after all, he's an orphan!" It's not the kids' fault that you were divorced or widowed in the first place—but that unfortunate circumstance doesn't mean they should be coddled all their lives. A spoiled brat with one parent isn't any more acceptable than a spoiled brat with two.

3. *You, as adults, know what the children need better than the children do.* You don't give them candy whenever they ask for it; you don't let them drive at fourteen just because they want to; so why should you let them keep you single just because they think they don't like your choice of spouse?

4. *The parents will help each other on request.* In any marriage a good response to each other's needs is essential, but it is even more vital in a remarriage with children to be each other's best ally and constant helper. If Mother is the real parent and is spending the evening straightening out discipline problems, Father should relieve her of some of the burden of housework—cleaning up after dinner, doing part of the laundry, bathing the younger children—so she is free to do what only she can do. And if Mother is dealing with a situation where her children are flatly disobedient and she openly asks Father's help, he should be there—not to take over but to prove to the children that their nastiness doesn't drive Mom and Dad apart, it brings them closer together. "You're all against me," the child will cry, but pretty soon he will start finding ways to accommodate the situation.

5. *Both parents will be understanding and patient with the high demands of the children.* If you recognize, before marriage, that the children usually will be the greatest difficulty in the way of your success together, you will both be more understanding of the fact that when either parent spends extra time with the children instead of with the spouse, it is really for the spouse's sake. It works both ways: when the stepfather takes his stepson out to the ball game instead of taking his new wife to a movie, she should not be disappointed, because the closer the relationship between child and stepfather, the easier it will be for the marriage to work. Of course, if either parent spends all his or her time with the children, you don't have a marriage. There has to be a balance.

6. *Regardless of the children's complaints, the parents will have at least one night a week out with each other, without the children.* They may scream and weep and be rude to the babysitter, but you still have to have a chance to talk and have fun together, or you'll soon be strangers. When the children see that it isn't *every* night and that it will always be *one* night no matter how much they complain, they will almost always accommodate you in the end.

There will be other rules, of course—and new ones will be required as the need arises—but the better your communication about the problems in *advance*, the fewer the decisions you will have to make under stress. Following the rules will take enormous self-control, but that's part of being an adult. You just can't let the children manipulate you into acting childishly toward them or toward your new spouse.

Preparing the Way

If your first marriage was a serious step, your remarriage should be an even more serious one. Once you've decided whom you want to marry, you should be willing to take time to get things worked out before actually beginning your life together. If your new spouse refuses to wait, it speaks of immaturity and selfishness; the children need time to get used to him, and you need time to get used to the way he deals with you and the children. Does he get easily annoyed with them? Is he more demanding than giving? Is he afraid of them?

For remarriage to work, both spouses must be honest and open with each other, highly committed, loving, patient, and unselfish.

The extended engagement is more than a testing ground for your husband- or wife-to-be. It is also a chance for the children to get used to their parent's new mate. The children should have at least two or three months to get used to the *idea* of your remarriage before it actually happens. Even if they have known your intended spouse for months before you decide to get married, they will probably not have been thinking of him or her as a permanent resident of their home. With that new element added to the relationship, there has to be time for them to get accustomed to the coming change.

The more opportunities for contact between the children and their new stepparent, the better—provided these are in a positive context. It isn't enough for you to keep telling the kids how wonderful he is. Your love for him will only make them feel more threatened if they don't have a chance to reach their own positive feelings about him.

Talk to your children about your new spouse. Don't force them to suppress their negative feelings. If they don't like him at first, let them admit it, and be understanding about it. "He keeps trying to hold my hand," says your little girl. You shouldn't respond defensively ("He's going to be your new Daddy, so you have to let him"). Instead you should be helpful ("He just likes you a lot, but if you don't want him to, he'll stop for sure"). If you keep communication open with your children, you can help guide your new spouse into a relationship with them that will be comfortable for all concerned.

Of course, you should let your children know, right from the start, that there will be changes. You do the kids no favor if you say, "Don't worry—when Daddy and Jane are married, not a single thing will change." Children aren't usually fooled—they know there'll be changes. And the fact that you're lying about it may only worry them more.

It is much better to say, "The only thing I insist on is that you treat Jane nicely. If you don't want to talk to her, you don't have to, and if there are problems, we'll have plenty of time to work them out. Just come to me and tell me what's bothering you. But in the meantime, you are going to have to treat her politely and respectfully because she's going to be my wife, and that's only fair. I treat your friends nicely; you have to treat the people I love nicely, too."

If your children know that you aren't going to hate them because of their negative feelings toward your new spouse, a lot of anxiety will be eased. Because they can vent their fear and anger honestly with you, they won't have the need to do it subtly and viciously with her. They should also sense that you will respond to their reasonable requests. "I don't want her there at bedtime" shouldn't be dismissed abruptly with "She's *going* to be there, so get used to it!" The child is really saying, "I want to be with *just you* at bedtime." It's a plea for love and closeness. Treat it that way.

If you're the new spouse, of course, such rejections from the children can hurt. It can be humiliating when you feel loving toward a child and get repeatedly rejected. It takes great patience to not resent it for a long time when you kiss one of your stepchildren, and he loudly cries, "Yuck! Don't you kiss me!" But you can't afford to get angry. You have to say, kindly, "I didn't know it would bother you. I won't do it again until you want me to." You may shed more than a few tears and need more than a little building up from your mate after his or her children have put you down—but that's why you remarried, isn't it? To have that very comfort of knowing that someone loves you regardless of whether the kids or your business associates or anyone else is treating you nicely or not.

One thing that can help build bridges is to have a regular conference with each child every week—with *both* of you present. It should be a time when the child is encouraged to mention anything he wants to complain about, any unfairness, any grievances that he perceives from you or another child. These conferences help the child see the unity you are building in your marriage and help sponsor openness between him and the new parent. Also, it forestalls their manipulating the two of you. Children like to play one parent against the other in any family ("But Dad said I could!"), and in a new, fragile remarriage they can play the game even better. By having the grievances aired before both of you, they can't tell different stories to each parent. Most important, though, is that it gives the child a firm reminder that he holds a unique place in the family which is not the least bit threatened by the new marriage. In fact, his place is even firmer now that you are married.

Hold these conferences, if possible, on the same day every week, so that the child learns to count on them and feel secure with them.

Yours, Mine, and Ours

So far I've deliberately avoided getting into detail on the problem of remarriage when *both* of you have children. The problems are essentially the same, squared. Instead of one of you being a new parent, both of you are. The only new problem is that at least some of your kids will have conflicts with at least some of his or her kids.

Everything that applies if only one spouse brings children to the marriage applies here.

However, there is one important change: Before you marry, the two of you must review all your family rules and reconcile them. Bedtimes need to be adjusted so that his twelve-year-old is not going to bed before your ten-year-old; chores need to be fairly reassigned so that the children are expected to do an equal amount of work (based on age and situation); punishments need to be standardized so that you aren't putting a child on a week's restrictions when your new spouse only punished his child with fifteen minutes' confinement in a bedroom. In short, you must carefully calculate your unity right from the start so that when a child says, "You're not my mother! Dad wouldn't do it this way!" you can answer firmly, "Your father and I agreed that this is the way the rules are in this house. We explained that to you three weeks ago, and if you ask your father, he will tell you exactly the same thing." That statement must be true, or life together as a family will be impossible.

It is a good idea, however, in standardizing family practices, to make sure no child perceives a serious loss—you should even up the bedtimes by letting the twelve-year-old go to bed *later,* not by making the ten-year-old go to bed *earlier.* The first way, you make a friend of the older child; the second way, you make an enemy of the younger. Only in the area of chores should you probably increase demands to even things up. The more personal stake children are given in the duties of the household, as long as they see that no one is getting off easy, the more committed they will begin to feel to making the new alliance work.

What if some of your children don't get along with some of his or hers? Again, the only thing you should insist on is politeness. They aren't marrying each other, after all—they're only brought together because their parents are marrying. Encourage the kids to avoid quarrels and bring their grievances to their weekly interviews with both parents. Then make sure you take some kind of action to solve the problem so they get used to the idea that solutions come from *you,* not from yelling at or beating up on their new housemates.

Don't try to force the kids together all the time on the theory that it will make them learn to get along. In fact, it is a good idea to let each group of children have plenty of time alone with their real parent and their real brothers and sisters, to reaffirm the family ties that they have long counted on. The more secure they feel in their original family, the more easily they will learn to compromise and grow to feel affection toward the strangers who have moved in. And be scrupulously fair in dealing with both sets of children. Don't automatically believe your child's story and doubt his child's version of events. In fact, in solving quarrels it is far better simply to separate the kids and wait until tempers have cooled before trying to solve the dispute. The children must learn quickly that they will be treated by the same rules, with no favoritism at all.

In combining families, your children will have many fears about the marriage before it happens. Be ready with answers. Will they have to move? Will they change schools? Will they have to share a room with a stranger or give up their private bedroom? Will their allowance change? What if the other kids want to watch a different TV show at the same time? Will your kids have to share their toys or bikes all the time, whether they want to or not?

Before the wedding make sure there are plenty of chances for the two groups of kids to combine, involuntarily if necessary, but in happy circumstances. They'll gladly go to the amusement park, even if they have to do it with "those other kids," and they probably won't stay home from a movie, either. Don't force them to kiss each other or even talk to each other—they're used to choosing their own friends. But do insist that they get used to having each other around so they can get a sense of what to expect and how to cope when they're living together. If you make reasonable demands of your children—courtesy, for instance—they'll be much more likely to come around on their own to the greater friendship and intimacy you would like to see them have. If you insist on that closeness from the start, you actually decrease the chance of their achieving it.

Successfully combining families is one of the hardest things you'll ever do. But if you go into it with the right spouse, with your eyes wide open, and with great stores of patience and a lot of mutual support, it is possible to make it work. I've seen it happen many times. Just withhold your judgment for a year or two. The problems that seem insurmountable the first year are often gone by the second—if you deal with them properly. And if you find the challenge greater than you expected, don't hesitate to seek professional guidance. If ordinary first marriages often need outside help, how much more likely it is for family mergers to need help!

Remember that you didn't remarry for your immediate pleasure, but for your long-range happiness. You are going through that difficult first year for the sake of the happiness you'll have five to ten years down the line—and twenty years later, when all the kids are grown up and gone, and you and your husband or wife can sigh in relief and enjoy each other all the more because of the tremendous challenges you met successfully together.

PART 4

Summing Up

CHAPTER 24

Ten Keys for Making a
Good Marriage Great

There is nothing more important in life than the quality of our relationships with other people. And the key relationship which will most affect our happiness is that which we have with our husband or wife.

I would like to share with you what I believe are ten critical ideas about making a good marriage still better, maybe even great. These may appear disarmingly simple, but they all really work. And they work very powerfully.

FIRST KEY: *Shower Positives, Minimize Nagging.* When family conversation in large numbers of American homes was tape-recorded between four and seven in the evening and then analyzed, it was found that most of the communication was negative. Too often in family life it is the *mistakes* that catch our attention rather than what's *right.* And this is typically what happens in marriage. We focus on the 5 percent that is wrong with our partner, too often overlooking so much more that is right and good. Thus it is extremely important that we praise them or shower positives on them for the things that we most appreciate.

The law of reinforcement says, "Whatever behavior (in your spouse) you positively reinforce will tend to be repeated." And it will! Nagging, on the other hand, too often generates resistance in our partner. And frequently it produces behavior that is exactly the opposite of what we had originally desired. Shower positives! Acknowledge whatever your partner does that pleases you, again and again! I guarantee an absolutely terrific payoff for you if this is done on a consistent, honest basis.

SECOND KEY: *Let Your Spouse Know the Facilitators of Love.* Too often one spouse in a relationship will expect their partner to read their mind: that is, to know automatically, with little or no communication, what their most important need, want, or thought is. Because most of us are not mind readers, many of our needs and wants may remain unfulfilled. Let your spouse know what you want, what you need. Say it openly but also good naturedly, not as a threat or a demand. If you do, you'll get what you want 75 percent of the time. But remember, you have to say it out loud. Most people can't guess what you are thinking. But this applies, most importantly, the other way too! You need to know, accurately, what your spouse needs from you. You may have to ask—more than once—to find out. Then give them what they want! In most instances spouses do not urgently want twenty or thirty things from their partner. It is usually just one or two things that are critical for them. And they are usually things that can be easily given. Give them! If you do this regularly, it will dramatically change your marriage for the better!

THIRD KEY: *Defuse Anger.* Unchecked escalating anger can lead to battles, spouse abuse, and divorce. Strategies for checking anger include taking brief time-outs (go to the bathroom—it's a neutral, safe place); identifying the particular triggers of each other's anger responses, then avoiding or modifying them in the future; creating an anger diary after each outburst to more accurately identify high-risk situations; using humor to deflate anger (if used appropriately, it can totally change an explosive situation); talking to yourself to maintain control; or writing notes to each other rather than discussing or fighting over a hot issue. Don't discuss or negotiate touchy issues when you are hungry (low blood sugar), excessively fatigued, or on a vulnerable PMS day. Avoid "you are" or "you did" statements of blame—these are guaranteed to close down your communications no matter how right you are: you may win the battle but lose the war every time. You also might try deep breathing and relaxation exercises (wherever you are) to block the anger cycle and control intense emotions, and try answering provocative comments with a soft, calm voice. This can be rehearsed beforehand or actually role-played and can be very effective in teaching you how to block or interrupt anger outbursts. See chapter 11 for details on all of these techniques.

FOURTH KEY: *Positive Sexuality.* Long-term, good sex powerfully reinforces the pair-bond between husband and wife, helps heal wounds in the relationship, and enhances the self-esteem of both partners. It also reduces the chances of infidelity or seeking affection from others and provides the possibility of conceiving new life and creating one's own family. Even though there are many physical as well as psychological blocks that can impair one's capacity to love in a sexual way, the good news is that nearly all of these can be treated and overcome. There is no need for most people in good health not to have an excellent adjustment in this important area. Quality sex is also greatly enhanced by having an overall good relationship in other areas of your marriage. And this takes energy, commitment, planning, and positive communications to happen.

FIFTH KEY: *The Power of Commitment—Love Is a Daily Decision.* In many years of working with couples and families in conflict I have come to the conclusion that the single most important predictor of a couple's making their marriage last and avoiding the divorce court is commitment, not compatibility. Start out as mismatched as you want—if both partners have a strong desire to make the marriage work, it can still work and maybe even work very well. Struggle? Yes. But there can still be a remarkable amount of happiness in such unions. More than you would ever guess. I have seen it happen many times. And with time there can be a gradual merging of two quite different personalities into a reciprocal whole. A couple can make it happen by having a clear intention of what they want to create, through their focused energy and will.

In other words, I see increasing evidence that it is possible with commitment to make nearly any marriage succeed (with a few important exceptions). The mistaken notion that you had to marry the "right one" sent some individuals on a mistaken chase through many relationships or marriages seeking something resembling perfection. In most cases all they got was disappointment. Perfection in love relationships does not exist. And while it is certainly true that some badly flawed individuals with abusive personalities make for bad spouses, there are still many divorces that need never have happened. Married love is not courtship love but can be much more profound, stable, deeper, and much less fickle. A couple may act as either healing agents for each other or as abusive enemies. And whether they are the one or the other comes from a freely made choice, a commitment to love. I am convinced that love is a daily decision. Love is action. For it to last it has to be demonstrated daily in a hundred ways. You choose to love. It doesn't just somehow happen. You create it. It is *your* responsibility. No one else's.

SIXTH KEY: *Develop Effective Communication and Negotiation Skills.* Surprisingly, skills in these areas can be learned and quickly improved on. Since every married couple brings a variety of differences to the relationship, this necessarily means that in all marriages there will be occasional disagreement and even conflict. So the key issue in having a happy, successful marriage is developing, to a fine art, skill in negotiating through one's differences. Successful time-proven techniques for negotiation are given in detail in chapters 4 and 11.

SEVENTH KEY: *The "Extra Dimension."* This refers to the influence of God, whom I believe has a great investment in our being successful and happy in our marriages. He created and sanctified this special institution. And just as God healed the sick and made the blind see, I believe that it is possible for relationships—through a divine influence—to be similarly healed, anger and hatred dissolved, and for forgiveness and renewal to occur. If the couple chooses to petition for such influence and assistance in their relationship, God will help them.

EIGHTH KEY: *Acute Stress Can Kill Love—Deal with It!* Acute stress from any source can greatly diminish our power to love each other. Sometimes couples mistakenly blame each other, as a personal thing, for being indifferent, unloving, less sexual, more irritable or less courteous compared to an earlier point in their marriage or courtship when things were going better. In reality, the true culprit often is severe stress in the life of either or both partners. This may come from almost any source inside or outside the relationship. It might be an impossible job situation, a failing business, health problems, living with an extremely difficult child, a financial crisis, intense pain, or chronic illness. Thus, it could be one of these that is actually poisoning the well in your marriage, not a true failing of commitment to the relationship. The solution involves reducing the stress any way you can or remaining patient until circumstances change and things get better in your or your partner's life. To leave under these circumstances could be unwise because the same thing might soon occur in your next marriage or relationship. It is extremely important in these situations that you not incorrectly blame the marriage as the major source of your or their inability to be as loving and caring as in the past. But you still need to deal with and move through the stress in order to free up energy for the most important relationship in your life. And if receiving outside counseling might offer you solutions, don't hesitate to get it.

NINTH KEY: *Participate in a Marriage Enrichment or Marriage Encounter Experience.* This is one of the most powerful loving and healing experiences that I know of. And it is something that can be done again and again. It is like a great big valentine that you can give to your spouse (and yourself!), and it can happen at any time of the year. Among other things, it focuses very powerfully on improving your communication skills together. It's very safe, inexpensive, and something you deserve. See chapter 9 for details.

TENTH KEY: *Pair-bonding, Renewing the Magic.* In some marriages couples become "married singles" who live in the same house together, but the excitement, romance, and intimacy of their early courtship and honeymoon years have long shriveled up and blown away. This need not be the case. As a longtime counselor of couples the most exciting thing I see is couples changing, growing, regenerating their relationship, and regaining the magic they once had. Pair-bonding occurs through making a daily decision to love, persisting in that decision, using the "I change first rule" (see chapter 6), improving each other's self-esteem, showering positives on each other, and taking daily time to share feelings (not solve problems, that's for another time). Then, like a giant 747, your relationship can become airborne again, doing something which appeared at one time almost impossible. This recreation of pair-bonding I've seen happen hundreds of times. This is what this book is about. And how to achieve it, if you want it. Life is a journey. And it might as well be an exhilarating journey. It's your choice.

EXTRA BONUS KEY: *The Forty-Eight-Hour Retreat.* Our experience has suggested that every couple needs periodic breaks from the acute stress of everyday living to strengthen their love, improve communication, plan for the future, and renew their marriage vows. This can be a downtown hotel on a weekend when rates are low or at a nearby resort area out-of-season. Leave behind your job, kids, and jangling phone in order to give your relationship number-one priority. This gives you time to make love, play, dine well, and renew your friendship unhassled by outside pressures. One couple I know accomplished the same thing at almost no expense by pitching a tent in a nearby wilderness area and having a joyous renewal in their own Garden of Eden. In another instance a physician (who worked seventy-hour weeks) kept the sizzle in his romance with his wife by having forty-eight-hour retreats away from home every third weekend. To them it was almost like a monthly honeymoon. As his wife put it, it was a wonderful opportunity to renew their intimacy and experience a rebonding of their relationship. On these occasions they were able to enjoy each other's company with no interruptions or interfering phone calls. They made plans for the future, discussed their children's needs, healed any hurts or disappointments, played together, and enjoyed superb physical intimacy during prime-time hours. But for this to work, it has to occur regularly, not just once a year.

References

CHAPTER 1. The Impossible Dream: Beginning the Journey

Freedman, J. *Happy People*. Cited in *Marriage Enrichment*, May 1986.

Gilder, George. *Naked Nomads, Unmarried Men in America*. New York: Quadrangle Books, 1974.

Glenn, N. D., and L. N. Weaver. "The Contributions of Marital Happiness to Global Happiness." *Journal of Marriage and the Family*. February 1981.

National Center for Health Statistics. *Annual Summary of Births, Marriages, Divorces and Deaths: U.S. 1984*. Vol. 33, No. 13, U.S. Dept. of Health and Human Services. September 1985.

CHAPTER 2. What Every Wife Wants from Her Husband

Dobson, J. *What Wives Wish Their Husbands Knew About Women*. Wheaton, Ill.: Tyndale House Publishers, Inc., 1975.

Lauer, J., and R. Lauer. "Marriages Made to Last." *Psychology Today*, June 1985.

Reik, T. *Sex in Man and Woman: Its Emotional Variations.* New York: Farrar, Straus and Cudahy, Inc., 1960.

CHAPTER 3. What Every Husband Wants from His Wife

Rubin, T. I. "What Makes a Woman Lovable." *Ladies' Home Journal,* June 1969.

CHAPTER 4. Communication Skills and Beyond

Bellack, A. S., and M. Hersan. *Research and Practice in Social Skills Training.* New York: Plenum Press, 1979.

Brandt, A. "Avoiding Couple Karate: Lessons in the Martial Arts." *Psychology Today,* October 1982.

Broderick, C. *Couples.* New York: Simon & Schuster, 1979.

Garland, D. R. "Training Married Couples in Listening Skills: Effects on Behavior, Perceptual Accuracy and Marital Adjustments." *Family Relations,* 30, 1981, 297–306.

Gottman, J., C. Notarius, J. Gonso, and H. Markman. *A Couples Guide to Communication.* Champaign, Ill.: Research Press, 1976.

Hammond, C., D. H. Hepworth, and V. G. Smith. *Improving Therapeutic Communication.* San Francisco: Jossey-Bass Publishers, 1977.

Montgomery, B. M. "The Form and Function of Quality Communication in Marriage." *Family Relations,* 30, 1981, 21–30.

Robbins, J., ed. *The Good Marriage: It Doesn't Just Happen.* Pleasantville, N.Y.: Sunburst Communications, 1978 (three filmstrips and cassettes).

CHAPTER 5. Sexual Love That Lasts: What It Takes

Annon, J. S. *Behavioral Treatment of Sexual Problems.* New York: Harper & Row, 1976.

Grace, M., and J. Grace. *A Joyful Meeting—Sexuality in Marriage.* St. Paul, Minn.: International Marriage Encounter, 1980.

Kaplan, H. S. *The New Sex Therapy.* New York: Brunner/Mazel, 1974.

LaHay, T., and B. LaHay. *The Act of Marriage.* Grand Rapids: Zondervan, 1976.

Masters, W. H., and V. Johnson. *The Pleasure Bond.* Boston: Little, Brown & Co., 1970.

Masters, W. H., V. Johnson, and R. C. Kolodny. *Masters and Johnson on Sex and Human Loving.* Boston: Little, Brown & Co., 1985.

CHAPTER 6. Pair-Bonding: Renewing the Magic

Branden, N. *The Psychology of Romantic Love: What Love Is, Why Love Is Born, Why It Sometimes Grows, Why It Sometimes Dies.* Los Angeles: Tarcher, 1980.

Hine, J. R. *What Comes after You Say, "I Love You"?* Palo Alto: Pacific Books, 1980.

Mace, D., and V. Mace. "What Is Marriage Beyond Living Together?: Some Quaker Reactions to Cohabitation." *Family Relations,* 30, January 1981, 17–20.

Schwartz, G., and D. Merten. *Love and Commitment.* Beverly Hills: Sage, 1980.

Stuart, R. B. *Helping Couples Change.* New York: The Guilford Press, 1980.

CHAPTER 8. Personal Energy and Health: Keeping in Shape

Growdon, J. H. "Neurotransmitter Precursors in the Diet: Their Use in the Treatment of Brain Disease." In *Nutrition and the Brain. Vol. 3, Disorders of Eating and Nutrients in Treatment of Brain Disease,* edited by R. J. Wurtman and J. J. Wurtman. New York: Raven Press, 1979.

Lipton, M. A., et al. "Vitamins, Megavitamin Therapy and the Nervous System." In *Nutrition and the Brain. Vol. 3, Disorders of Eating and Nutrients in Treatment of Brain Disease,* edited by R. J. Wurtman and J. J. Wurtman. New York: Raven Press, 1979.

Prevention Magazine Health Academy Service. "The Stanford University Guide to a Healthier Heart." *Prevention,* February 1986.

Wurtman, R. J., and J. J. Wurtman. eds. *Nutrition and the Brain, Vol. 4: Toxic Effects of Food Constituents on the Brain.* New York: Raven Press, 1979.

CHAPTER 9. Marriage Encounter and Marriage Enrichment: The Super Experience

Demarest, D., J. Sexton, and M. Sexton. *Marriage Encounter.* St. Paul, Minn.: National Marriage Encounter, 1977.

Mace, D. and V. Mace. *We Can Have Better Marriages if We Really Want Them.* Nashville: Abingdon, 1974.

Mace, D. and V. Mace. *How to Have a Happy Marriage.* Nashville: Abingdon, 1977.

Otto, H., ed. *Marriage and Family Enrichment: New Perspectives and Programs.* Nashville: Abingdon, 1976.

CHAPTER 10. The Extra Dimension

Lenski, G. *The Religious Factor.* Garden City, N.Y.: Doubleday, 1961.

CHAPTER 11. Defusing Anger: Handling Differences and Conflicts

Hoopes, M. "Resolution of Family Conflict." *Family Perspective,* Spring 1973.

Jacobson, N., and G. Margolin. *Marital Therapy: Strategies Based on Social Learning and Behavior Exchange Principles.* New York: Brunner/Mazel, 1979.

Menninger, C. W., with M. Lane. "What Wives Can Do to Solve the Communication Problem." *Woman's Day,* May 1969.

Novaco, R. W. "Stress Inoculation for Anger Control." In *Innovations in Clinical Practice: A Source Book,* edited by P. A. Keller and L. G. Ritt, Vol. 2. Sarasota, Florida: Professional Resource Exchange, Inc. 1983.

Novaco, R. W. "Anger Control Therapy." In *Dictionary of Behavior Therapy Techniques,* edited by A. S. Bellack and L. G. Ritt. Elmsford, N.Y.: Pergamon Press Inc., 1985.

Stuart, R. B. *Helping Couples Change.* New York: The Guilford Press, 1980.

Tavris, C. *Anger: The Misunderstood Emotion.* New York: Simon & Schuster, 1983.

Wright, H. N. "Helping Couples Resolve Conflict Problems." *Marital Counseling.* New York: Harper & Row, 1983.

CHAPTER 12. The Immature Partner: Lazy, Irresponsible, and Selfish

Kanfer, F. H., and A. P. Goldstein, eds. *Helping People Change: A Textbook of Methods.* 2d ed. New York: Pergamon Press, 1980.

CHAPTER 13. Surviving with a Jealous Spouse

Constantine, L. L. "Jealousy: From Theory to Intervention," in D. H. Olson, ed. *Treating Relationships.* Lake Mills, Iowa: Graphic Publishing Co., 1976.

Salovey, P., and J. Rodin. "The Heart of Jealousy." *Psychology Today,* September 1985.

CHAPTER 14. Coping with Violence

Bard, M. "The Study and Modification of Intra-Familial Violence." *The Control of Aggression and Violence: Cognitive and Physiological Factors,* edited by J. L. Singer. New York: Academic Press, 1971.

Dobash, R. E. and R. Dobash. *Violence against Wives.* New York: The Free Press, 1979.

Gelles, R. J. *Family Violence: Sage Library of Social Research,* Vol. 84. Beverly Hills: Sage, 1979.

Moore, D. M. *Battered Women.* Beverly Hills: Sage Publications, 1979.

Straus, M. A. and G. T. Hotaling, eds. *The Social Causes of Husband-Wife Violence.* Minneapolis: Univ. of Minnesota Press, 1980.

Walker, L. E. *The Battered Woman.* New York: Harper & Row, 1979.

CHAPTER 15. Cheating and Infidelity: When Trust Is Broken

Barbeau, C. C. *The Joy of Marriage.* Minneapolis, Minn.: Winston Press, Inc., 1976.

Benson, Herbert, with Miriam Z. Klipper. *The Relaxation Response.* New York: Avon Books, 1979.

Broderick, C. *Couples.* New York: Simon & Schuster, 1979.

Kreitler, P., with B. Bruns. *Affair Prevention.* New York: The Macmillan Publishing Co., 1981.

Masters, W. H., and V. Johnson. *The Pleasure Bond.* Boston: Little, Brown & Co., 1970.

Masters, W. H., V. Johnson, and R. C. Kolodny. *Masters and Johnson on Sex and Human Loving.* Boston: Little, Brown & Co., 1985.

McCary, J. L. *Freedom and Growth in Marriage.* New York: John Wiley & Sons, 1980.

McGinnis, T. "An Innovative Strategy for Treating Extramarital Affairs." In *Innovations in Clinical Practice: A Source Book. Vol. 3,* edited by P. A. Keller and L. G. Ritt. Sarasota, Fla.: Professional Resource Exchange, Inc., 1984.

O'Neill, N. *The Marriage Premise.* New York: Bantam Books, 1977.

Pietropinto, A., and J. Simenauer. *Husbands and Wives.* New York: Times Books, 1979.

Sager, C. J., and B. Hunt. *Intimate Partners.* New York: McGraw-Hill, 1979.

Saxton, L. *The Individual, Marriage and the Family.* 4th ed. Belmont, Calif.: Wadsworth Publishing Co., 1980.

Singer, L. J. *Stages: The Crises that Shape Your Marriage.* New York: Grossett & Dunlap, 1980.

Venditti, M. C. *How to Be Your Own Marriage Counselor.* New York: Continuum Publishing Corp., 1980.

CHAPTER 16. The Partner Who Abuses Alcohol or Drugs

Delehanty, E. J. *The Therapeutic Value of the Twelve Steps of A.A.* Salt Lake City: Utah Alcoholism Foundation.

Kaplan, H. I., and B. J. Sadock. *Comprehensive Textbook of Psychiatry.* 4th ed. Baltimore: Williams & Wilkins, 1985.

Klein, D. F., and R. Gitteiman-Klein. *Progress in Psychiatric Drug Treatment.* New York: Brunner/Mazel, 1975.

Knowles, P. "Diagnosis and Treatment Decisions for Alcohol and

Substance Abusers." In *Innovations in Clinical Practice: A Source Book, Vol. 3,* edited by P. A. Keller and L. G. Ritt. Sarasota, Fla.: Professional Resource Exchange, Inc., 1984.

Manatt, M. *Parents Peers and Pot.* Rockville, Md: U.S. Public Health Service, National Institute on Drug Abuse, 1979.

Miller, W. R., and R. F. Munoz. *How to Control Your Drinking.* Albuquerque: Univ. of New Mexico Press, 1982.

Royce, J. E. *Alcohol Problems and Alcoholism.* New York: The Free Press, 1981.

Sue, D., et al. *Understanding Abnormal Behavior.* Boston: Houghton Mifflin Co., 1986.

Van Praag, H. M. *Psychotropic Drugs.* New York: Brunner/Mazel, 1978.

CHAPTER 17. Depression in the Relationship: What to Do

Fann, W. E., et al, eds. *Phenomenology and Treatment of Depression.* New York: Spectrum Publishing, Inc., 1977.

Greist, J. and T. H. Greist. *Antidepressant Treatment—The Essentials.* Baltimore: Williams & Wilkins, 1979.

Kaplan, H. I. and B. J. Sadock. *Comprehensive Textbook of Psychiatry,* 4th ed. Baltimore: Williams & Wilkins, 1985.

Kline, N. S. *From Sad to Glad.* New York: Ballantine Books, 1981.

Lewinsohn, P. M., et al. *Control Your Depression.* Englewood Cliffs, N. J.: Prentice-Hall, Inc., 1978.

CHAPTER 18. Living with a Neurotic or Emotionally Unstable Spouse

Schumer, F. *Abnormal Psychology.* Lexington, Mass.: D.C. Health Co., 1983.

CHAPTER 19. Psychological Allergies in Marriage: The Poison Ivy Spouse

Smedes, L. B. *Forgive and Forget.* New York: Harper and Row, Publishers, Inc., 1984.

CHAPTER 20. Premenstrual Syndrome: Some Days Can Be Tough

Cannon, P., and D. C. Hammond. "Periodic Madness: Identifying and Treating PMS." *AMCAP Journal*, November 1985.

Colbert, T. "What is PMS?" *The PMS Connection* (Newsletter of PMS Action, Madison, Wisconsin), 1983.

Dalton, K. *Once a Month: The Premenstrual Syndrome*. Pomona, Calif.: Hunter House, Inc., 1979.

Horrobin, D. F. "The Importance of Gamma-Linolenic Acid and Prostaglandin El in Human Nutrition and Medicine." *Journal of Holistic Medicine*. Vol. 3, No. 2, Fall/Winter 1981.

Kaplan, H. I., and B. J. Sadock. *Comprehensive Textbook of Psychiatry* (Vol. 4). Baltimore: Williams & Wilkins, 1985.

Mazer, E. "There's New Help for Those Monthly Blues." *Prevention*, August 1983.

Northrup, C. *Women's Bodies, Women's Wisdom*. New York: Bantam Books, 1994.

CHAPTER 21. Deciding on Divorce: Should I Stay and Suffer or Leave and Die?

Adam, J., and N. Adam. *Divorce*. Englewood Cliffs, N. J.: Prentice-Hall, Inc., 1979.

Cline, V. *How to Make Your Child a Winner*. New York: Walker & Co., 1980.

Edwards, J. N., and J. M. Saunders. "Coming Apart: A Model of the Marital Dissolution Decision." *Journal of Marriage and the Family*. May 1981.

Glenn, N. D., and B. K. Kramer. "The Psychological Wellbeing of Adult Children of Divorce." *Journal of Marriage and the Family*. November 1985.

Levinger, G., and O. C. Moles. *Divorce and Separation: Context, Causes, and Consequences*. New York: Basic Books, 1979.

Mace, D. "When Children of Divorce Grow Up." *Marriage Enrichment*, Vol. 14, No. 3, March 1986.

CHAPTER 22. Choosing the Right One

Block, J. D. *To Marry Again.* New York: Grosset and Dunlap, 1979.

Larson, J. "Remarriage: Myths, Realities, and Complexities." *Family Life.* Vol. L, No. 6, November and December 1980.

Messinger, L. "Remarriage Between Divorced People with Children from Previous Marriages: A Proposal for Preparation for Remarriage." *Journal of Marriage and Family Counseling,* Vol. 2, No. 2, April 1976.

CHAPTER 24. Ten Keys for Making a Good Marriage Great

Trotter, R. J. "The Three Faces of Love." *Psychology Today.* September 1986.

Index